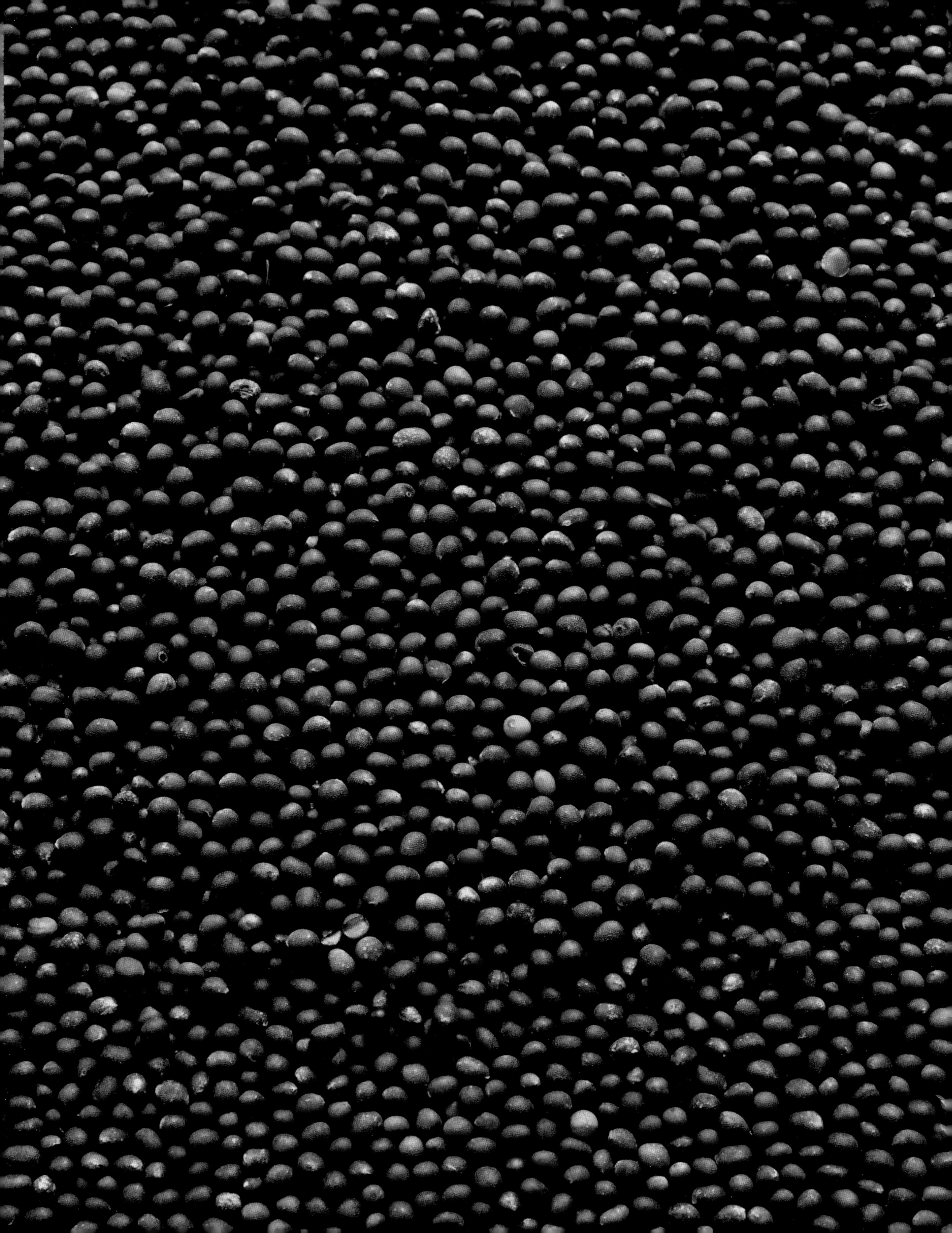

MAILLE

MAISON FONDÉE EN 1747

Recipes Jean-Pierre Biffi
Texts Cécile Maslakian
Photographs Iris Nara Miller
Styling Nathalie Nannini
Food styling Virginie Michelin

STEWART TABORI & CHANG | NEW YORK

PREFACE

STÉPHANE BERN

*M*ustard has lent its unmistakable flavour to dishes that have been endorsed by some of Europe's most illustrious figures and time itself. A flavour so loved that royal courts deemed it necessary to designate official suppliers. Their choice of supplier was based on a certain expertise passed down from generation to generation and in return, these purveyors were rewarded with a royal warrant for good and loyal service to the court. To become an official supplier is the ultimate recognition of quality and excellence. It is also a duty as well as an honour, a title to live up to at all times. In France, there is no association for the old and illustrious houses of excellence whose products were once served at the tables of kings and queens. However, I remember being at a gourmet literary dinner one day and noticing a particular date written on a stoneware jar, 1747, under the name of the most famous brand of mustard: Maille. When I tried this delicious old style mustard, with its unmistakable and delightful whole mustard seeds, I immediately thought of the expertise dating back to the 18th century that had gone into making it. It is human nature to look back at history with fondness and this affection for the past often makes us choose a product that has stood the test of time, such as an old style mustard that was once preferred by Louis XV and his mistress the Marquise de Pompadour. My curiosity for La Maison Maille was born that day when I scooped out the precious wholegrains to flavour my roast meat. It was when I became fascinated with the incredible culinary story of Antoine-Claude Maille, distiller and vinegar-maker, who opened his first master vinegar shop in Paris in 1747 and was to become an official purveyor to the court of Louis XV. How could I not be intrigued by such an artisan whole skills opened the doors of Versailles? In 1769, he became official vinegar-maker to His Majesty the King, a title that allowed La Maison Maille to also become official supplier to the royal courts of Austria and Russia. Maille mustard was also deemed worthy to represent France at the table of Queen Victoria of England. This book tells the amazing human and gastronomic story of mustard and vinegar. These two condiments may be common today, but Maille ensured they will always be held in the highest regard by making them a permanent symbol of sophistication, excellence and France's food culture. And in response to the ever-evolving tastes of consumers and gourmet trends, Maille has relied on its history to adapt to its current generation, continually reinventing itself, adding new flavours and creating innovative products, without ever losing the quality and qualities that made its name. True to Maille's philosophy, tradition should never hinder creativity and the gourmet recipes in these pages will take you on a gastronomic journey that combines culinary artistry and the soul of a globally loved product. A journey enhanced, as always, by Maille condiments.

XV,

du Roy »

ssie,

Prusse

TABLE OF CONTENTS

OF MAILLE

AND MEN

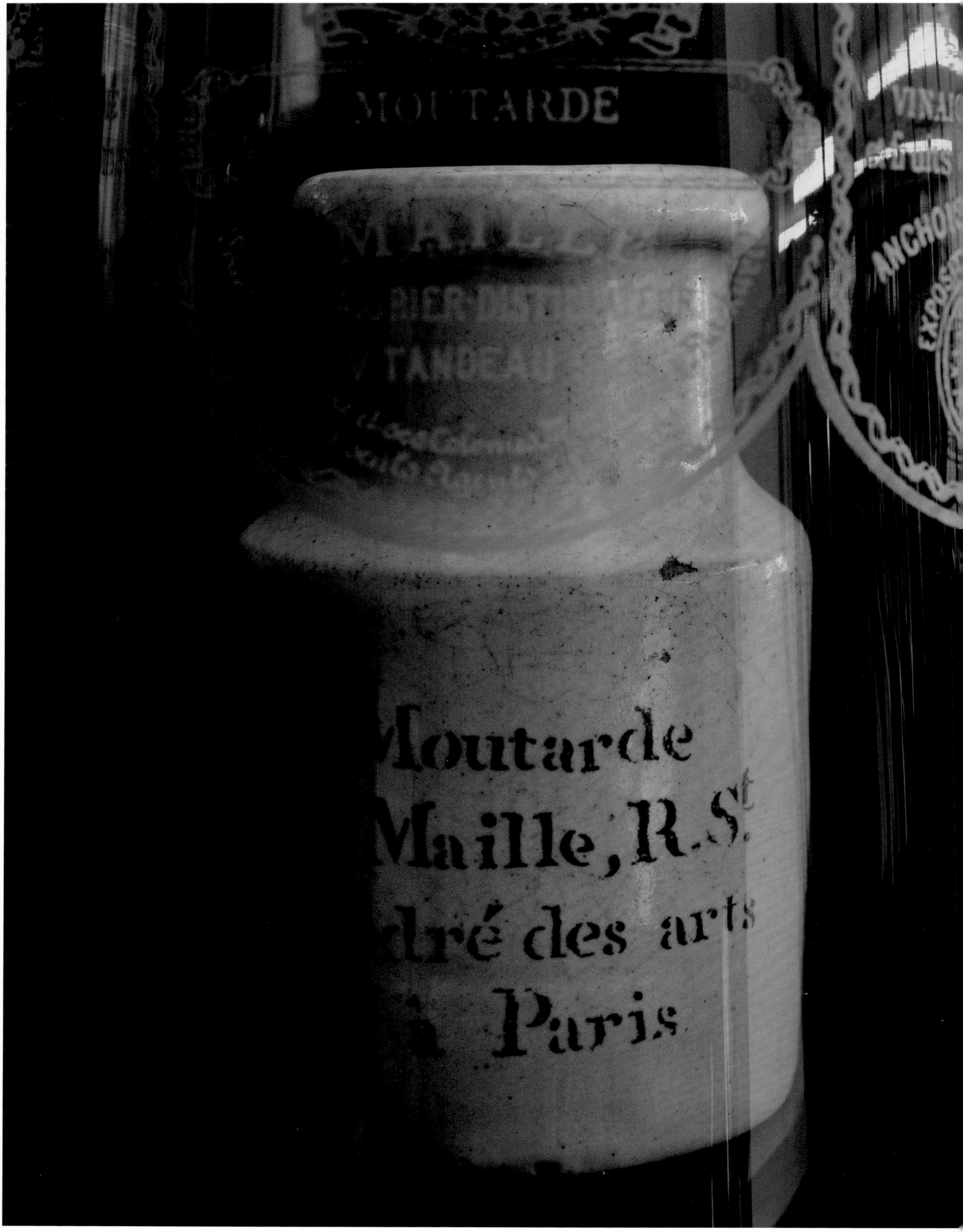
MOUTARDE
Moutarde
Maille, R. St
dré des arts
Paris

A teaspoon of honey mustard and a few drops of balsamic vinegar of Modena
in a marinade, a passion fruit and mandarin vinaigrette sprinkled over a salad,
a tender steak tartar topped with crunchy cornichons... sometimes it only takes
a condiment to turn good into extraordinary. It is often as simple as that. Subtle flavour
and texture combinations come together to create just the right sensory balance.

*L*a Maison Maille has been enhancing everyday meals and adding flavour to the daily lives of the French for almost three centuries, playing an influential role in establishing the country's famous food culture.

A contemporary of Louis XV, Antoine-Claude Maille the elder was a distiller and vinegar-maker based in Paris and made his name in 1720 by inventing Vinegar of the Four Thieves. He subsequently won some of the most prestigious of customers, including the Duke of Orleans, brother of Louis XIV, and the Marquise de Pompadour, mistress to King Louis XV. The family continued to be successful and in 1769 Antoine-Claude Maille the younger was awarded the title of official vinegar-maker by King Louis XV. At around the same time, La Maison Maille became the official supplier to the courts of Austria, Hungary, Russia and England. And so with its reputation established, La Maison Maille created a name for itself and also a legacy that successive managers have faithfully continued, ensuring that the company remains one of the leading fine-food purveyors in the world.

Two and a half centuries later, renowned international chefs and fine-food lovers have replaced kings by embracing Maille mustards and vinegars in their search for culinary perfection. Maille is the ideal partner for these gourmet artists, whose creativity is fed and stimulated by the range of exquisite flavours and textures that result from Maille's unique manufacturing process and unrivalled expertise.

Ever since a widespread enthusiasm for cooking appeared in the early 2000s, household kitchens have followed top restaurants by adding a certain creativity to meals. With Maille, a chef's hat is not required to enhance a sauce or homemade dish with a touch of honey mustard and balsamic vinegar, or a dash of vinegar with mango purée. A judicious pairing of a vegetable, meat, fish or even a fruit, and a carefully selected condiment can create the finest of dishes. The fact that people reach for mustards, vinegars and pickles on a daily basis is proof of this.

To see Maille products so well rooted in modern times, it is easy to forget that the earliest vinegar recipes date from the first century AD and it was discovered by accident more than 5000 years ago. When an alcohol is left in an open jar for a few days, it ferments and takes on a sour taste, resulting in vinegar. But this discovery still had to be exploited successfully. Again, it was by accident that the ability of this *vin aigre* (sour wine) to preserve foods was discovered. The medical world was quick to take interest in this discovery and began to use vinegar for its antiseptic and antibacterial properties, and as a remedy for many illnesses and injuries. In the Middle Ages, it was even used as an antidote for cooking supposedly poisonous foods before its value as a flavour enhancer was discovered.

Similarly, mustard also goes back several millennia. Three thousand years ago, the Chinese were already cultivating mustard seeds and probably eating them with their food. The Greeks and Egyptians subsequently helped to introduce the seeds throughout the Mediterranean basin. Much later, someone had the bright idea of grinding mustard seeds with vinegar, and mustard was born. But who was this person? And when was this discovery made? History reveals that in Roman times mustard was used in a similar form to how we know it today; that is, used as a paste to enhance the flavour of meat and vegetables, and for its therapeutic qualities. So the transformation from seed to paste must have happened at some point between the two eras. The Romans then introduced it to Gaul where we first encounter the word mustard (from the Latin words *mustum* and *ardens* meaning 'burning must') at the beginning of the 13th century. It had previously been known as *sinapis*. Over the centuries, the whole world was to experience the pleasures of mustard and many peoples invented their own mustard recipes.

In the 13th century under Saint-Louis, Parisian vinegar-makers were given permission to make mustard. In 1336, it was consumed in vast quantities during celebrations held by the Duke of Burgundy in honour of his cousin the King of France, Philippe VI of Valois. A few years later, in 1354, the receiver general of Burgundy had the ingenious idea of offering four barrels of Dijon mustard to King John and Queen Joan I of Auvergne, whose royal approval cemented the reputation of mustard from this region. But why Burgundy? Burgundy's many vineyards are perfect for producing verjuice, an acidic juice extracted from unripe grapes. The limestone lands around Burgundy are also ideal for growing mustard seeds. So this area has all the right conditions for a thriving mustard business. As a result, its popularity also thrived throughout the country.

As for the cucumbers used for gherkins, they originated in India. They were also cultivated in Egypt more

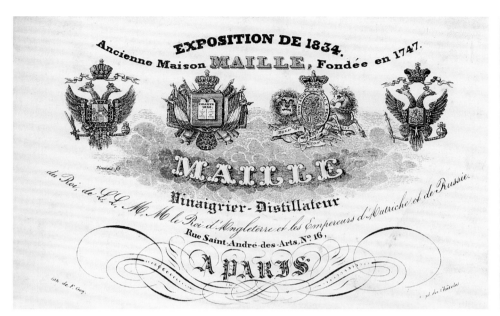

Above:
Publicity issued at the occasion of the French Public Industrial Products Exhibition in 1834.
'Vinegar, 1586', travelling vinegar salesman.

than 3000 years before they starting appearing on French tables in the Middle Ages. But it was not until the 20th century that they were taken to new heights by Maille, with its extra-fine and even mini versions, boasting unrivalled flavour and a firm, crunchy texture. Back in the 17th century, production of these condiments was regulated by master mustard- and vinegar-makers who were granted statutes to form their own guild in Dijon in 1634. Several years of apprenticeship followed by a tour of France were required before being admitted. The statutes granted them exclusive rights to make mustard and vinegar. In return, they were obliged to put their seal on barrels so that the source of any mustard could be traced back to the manufacturer. Later, Louis XIV granted them their own coat of arms, which they could engrave on their seals and display on their banners.

La Maison Maille was founded a century later under the leadership of Antoine-Claude Maille, a master vinegar-maker based in Paris. He quickly became the official supplier to King Louis XV. He was then allowed to associate the King's coat of arms to his own, thus creating the Maille coat of arms.

Almost three centuries of commercial and industrial innovation followed, along with numerous awards, markets entered and partnerships with the world's top chefs. This has resulted in La Maison Maille becoming a symbol of France's culinary heritage — a heritage that it continues to enrich and sustain. The first boutique opened its doors in Dijon in 1845 and a second followed in Paris in 1996. In early 2013, La Maison Maille started opening new stores and online boutiques around the world.

Its success is down to many talented men and women. In addition to Antoine-Claude Maille the elder and younger, numerous men and women have maintained and enhanced the reputation of the Maille name over the years, thus contributing to its status today as one of the finest suppliers of gourmet condiments in France and around the world.

THREE CENTURIES OF CULINARY INNOVATION

The creative genius of Antoine–Claude Maille, father and son

The 18th century was the Age of Enlightenment when discoveries and innovations in all fields were flourishing. It was also a time of great thinkers and philosophers. In this context, society turned towards the pursuit of better health, comforts and refinement of manners. This was a propitious time for Antoine-Claude Maille who seized this century's opportunities with passion, inspired by all the creativity around him and which became a part of his legacy. He was able to understand and exploit the changes and trends of his time, and so became one of the major players in his field.

The stroke of genius

At the beginning of the 18th century, Antoine-Claude Maille was a master vinegar-maker based on Rue de l'Hyrondelle in Saint-André-des-Arcs parish in Paris. His business was a modest success until a tragic event: in 1720, the great plague ravaged the city of Marseille. The epidemic appeared in June and claimed 500 lives per day in August, a figure that had doubled by September. There seemed to be no cure. The pandemic was to cause 50,000 deaths in one year. This was the perfect time for Antoine-Claude Maille to introduce his 'Vinegar of the Four Thieves' with its antiseptic properties.

The recipe was apparently disclosed by four thieves who were operating during the great plagues of Toulouse from 1628 to 1631. Lawless, but organised and cautious, they protected themselves from contamination by soaking a cloth with their vinegar recipe and applying it to the face. After being arrested and sentenced to be burned alive, they promised to disclose the recipe for their vinegar in return for a lighter sentence — which is what they did before being hanged! Whether this legend is true or not, we do know that a century later, Antoine-Claude Maille created his version of the vinegar and made it available to the people of Marseille, protecting them from contagion and saving many lives. His prescription was as follows: 'on an empty stomach, swallow a teaspoonful in a glass of water, rub on the temples and on the inside of hands'. This was the flash of brilliance that launched Maille vinegar, the starting point for a fascinating story.

A creative instinct passed from father to son

Taking over from his father of the same name, Antoine-Claude Maille the younger was registered as master vinegar-maker in 1742. He was to have a considerable impact on the brand.
To the 9 varieties of vinegar beauty product that his father created for women, he added no less than 92. Herbal vinegars, perfumed using plant and flower extracts, have been used for thousands of years as hair care products. The extracts were obtained by distillation of aromatic plants in a still.

Right: Robert Maille, son of Antoine-Claude Maille.

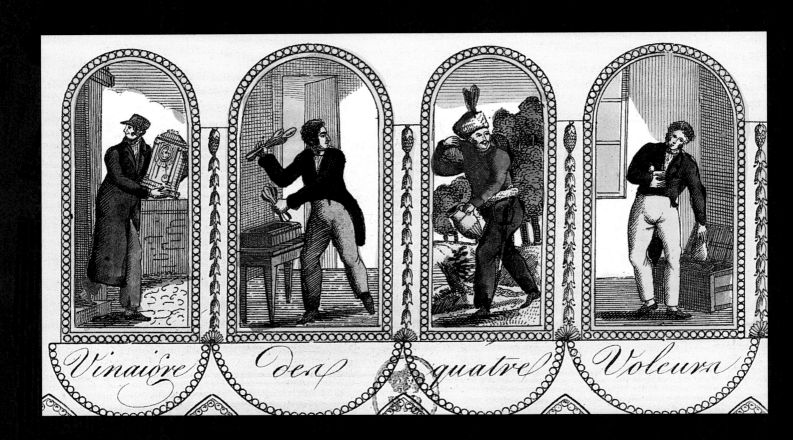

Vinaigre des quatre Voleurs

RECIPE FOR

'Vinegar
of the Four Thieves'

⌒

3 pints of strong white wine vinegar

A handful of wormwood, meadowsweet,
juniper seeds, wild marjoram, sage

50 cloves

2 ounces of campanula roots

2 ounces of angelica

2 ounces of rosemary

2 ounces of horehound

3 grams of camphor

who swore by these miraculous beautifying products. Each vinegar had its own special properties, including some rather extravagant ones, such as the 'virgin vinegar for the ladies', which was rather unique in that it had the ability to 'make husbands believe they are the first'. History does not reveal whether it received approval from the Royal Commission of Medicine or whether husbands were successfully fooled.

Because Antoine-Claude Maille was inspired by the kitchen as much as by beauty and health, he created an impressive amount of flavoured vinegars. They are mentioned in *La vie privée des Français* by Legrand d'Aussy. He lists 55 varieties of vinegar created by Maille: 'aniseed, imperial, marinated, strong red, distilled elderberry (...) savory, anchovies, capers...'. His 'catalogue' ultimately lists 175 types. He even made vinegar-based syrups which, once mixed with water from the Seine, made the water both healthier and tastier. The Parisian people were able to quench their thirst by drinking vinegar syrup flavoured with rose, lemon, orange flower or vanilla. With Antoine-Claude Maille's influence, the daily lives of many became that little bit more refined.

'The Maille name spread like wildfire among society's elite who swore by these miraculous beautifying products.'

In 1769, one of his inventions was literally on everyone's lips: a beautifying rouge. This anti-ageing cosmetic was ahead of its time, a vinegar-based beauty product that improved complexion, kept skin healthy and prevented lips from cracking. La Maison Maille made two varieties: a light one and dark one. They looked perfectly natural and never ran. Furthermore, the colour did not fade even at high temperatures. And when the mercury dropped, just a little of the light rouge rubbed on the lips would prevent chapping. Women were quickly converted and just as quickly spread the news. Driven by advertisements of the time and word-of-mouth — which was already the best of advertisements — the Maille name spread like wildfire among society's elite

On the business front, Antoine-Claude Maille also proved to be particularly ahead of his time. In 1747, the year La Maison Maille officially opened its first boutique, he published an advertisement in the *Mercure de France*, one of the most read newspapers at the time. This is what he wrote: 'The Public is hereby notified that Sir Maille possesses all the secrets for the distillation of vinegars and manufacturing of mustards'. Not quite as catchy as the now famous 'Maille mustard is my mustard', which is the English version of the original French *'Il n'y a que Maille qui m'aille'* coined almost two centuries later. Nevertheless, his advertisement worked and his store gained a certain notoriety.

Above: Mustard – vinegar maker's dress, 18th century.
Right: Rates of Maille and Aclocque vinegars and mustards, 1815.

MAILLE et ACLOCQUE,

Vinaigriers-Distillateurs du Roi et de LL. MM. les Empereurs d'Autriche et de Russie,

Rue Saint-André-des-Arcs, n.° 16, et rue Vivienne, n.° 16, A PARIS.

SEULS pour la Composition générale de toutes sortes de Vinaigres doubles distillés, concentrés et spiritualisés, alcalisés, et de toutes sortes de Vinaigres tant pour la Table que pour les Bains et Toilettes.

VINAIGRES POUR LA TABLE.

La Bouteille.

A l'estragon	2 75
Naturel, 2.e qualité	2 75
Surard	2 75
A l'ail	5 75
A l'aubépine	5 75
Au basilic	5 75
Au baume	5 75
A la capucine	5 75
Au céleri	5 75
Au cerfeuil	5 75
Aux champignons	5 75
A la christe-marine	5 75
A la ciboulette	5 75
A la civette	5 75
Aux cornichons	5 75
Aux échalottes	5 75
A l'épine-vinette	5 75
A l'estrag. S. Florentin	5 75
Au fenouil marin	5 75
A la framboise	5 75
Au fumet pour gibier	5 75
Au genièvre	5 75
Au gingembre	5 75
Aux herbes fines	5 75
Au laurier	5 75
Aux mûres	5 75
Naturel, 1re qualité	5 75
Aux oignons	5 75
A l'oseille	5 75
A la passe-pierre	5 75
Au piment rouge et bl.	5 75
A la pimprenelle	5 75
A la ravigote	5 75
A la rocambole	5 75
A la rose blanche	5 75
A la rose rouge	5 75
A la sarriette	5 75
A la sauge	5 75
Au serpolet	5 75
Des six simples	5 75
Au thym	5 75
Aux câpres	4 50
A la chicorée	4 50
Mariné	4 50
Aux mille fleurs	4 50
Muscat	4 50
Aux abricots	5
Aux anchois	5
Aux mille feuilles	5
Au senevé	5
A la bigarade	6
Aux cerises	6
A la choisi	6
Au citron	6
A la fleur d'orange	6
Aux pêches	6
Aux pistaches	6
A la polonaise	6
Aux truffes	6
A la cannelle	12
Au girofle	12
A la vanille	12
Au macis	15

VINAIGRES De Parfums et Aromatiques,

A l'usage des Bains et Toilettes, distillés au verre, et différens Vinaigres servant à des opérations chimiques.

La Bouteille.

A l'absinthe	5
A l'ail distillé	5
A l'angélique	5
Au baume franc	5
Au cochléaria	5
Au coq	5
Distillé	5
A l'estragon distillé	5
A l'hysope	5
A la lavande	5
A la marjolaine	5
A la mauve	5
Au muguet	5
Au macis	5
Au népéta	5
Rafraîchissant pour la garde-robe	5
Au raifort	5
Pour le rasoir	5
Au romarin	5
A la sauge	5
Au serpolet	5
Au sureau distillé	5
Au thym	5
Pour la toilette	5
Anisé	6
Aux barbeaux	6
A l'esprit-de-vin	6
De lavande à la favorite	6
Au lys	6
Aux mille feuilles	6
A l'origan	6
Au stœcas	6
Vulnéraire bl. et rouge	6
A l'acacia	7
A la bergamote	7
Au bouquet	7
Au citron	7
A la citronnelle	7
Au fenouil	7
A la fleur d'orange	7
A la giroflée	7
A l'héliotrope	7
Au jasmin d'Espagne	7
A la jonquille	7
De lavande ambrée	7
De lavande à la bergamote	7
A la menthe	7
Aux mille fleurs	7
Au myrte p.r les bains	7
Au néroli	7
A l'œillet d'Espagne	7
Au Portugal	7
Au pot-pourri	7
Aux roses balsamiques	7
Aux roses muscades	7
Au réséda	7
A la tubéreuse	7
A la violette	8
Au cédrat	8

Suite DES VINAIGRES De Parfums et Aromatiques.

La Bouteille.

De délices	8
Au passulat	8
Ambré	9
A l'américaine	9
A la belle Éléonore	9
A la créole	9
A la duchesse	9
De Hongrie	9
A la maréchale	9
Suave	9
Des sultanes	9
Au benjoin	12
A la cannelle	12
Concentré	12
Aux soucis	12
A la vanille	12
Musqué	12
Parfumé	12
Au macis	15
A la fleur de girofle	18
A la fleur de muscade	18
A la fleur d'épine	24
Philosophique	25
Au paracelse	48
Métallique	72

VINAIGRES DE PROPRIÉTÉS.

Vinagrillo d'Espague, le rouleau et le flacon	5
Blanc de Vinaigre, le pot	6
Lait de Vinaigre pour les masques de couche	6
Digestif	12
En flacon	5
Au millepertuis, pour enlever le rouge	12
En flacon	5
Au storax, qui blanchit la peau	12
En flacon	5
Alcalisé	12
En flacon	5
Anti-pestilentiel, pour chasser le mauvais air des appartemens	15
En flacon	5
Anti-scorbutique	15
En flacon	5
Camphré	15
En flacon	5
Des quatre voleurs	15
En flacon	5
Scillitique pour la voix	15
De Séville pour mouiller les tabacs de France et d'Espagne	15
En flacon	5
Astringent	24
En flacon	6
D'écaille, pour les dartres	24
En flacon	5

SUITE DES VINAIGRES de Propriétés.

A la fleur de citron, pour les boutons	24
En flacon	5
Fondant pour les cors aux pieds	24
En flacon	5
De perle	24
En flacon	5
Aux racines p.r enlever les taches de rousseur	24
En flacon	5
Romain qui blanchit les dents et guérit de la carie	24
En flacon avec la poudre	5
Styptique pour effacer les rides	24
En flacon	5
Au turbith pour guérir le mal de dents	24
En flacon	5
Admirable, sans pareil	36
En flacon	4 50
De beauté	36
En flacon	4 50
Pour la piqûre des cousins	36
En flacon	4 50
De Flore p.r éteindre les chaleurs de la peau	36
En flacon	4 50
De Vénus	96
En flac. avec le sel	4
DE ROUGE,	
1.re nuance, pâle	2 50
2.e nuance, foncé	3 50
3.e nuance, très-foncé	4 50

SELS DE VINAIGRES VOLATILS.

En petits Flacons.

Vinegar aromatic	6
Volatil	4
A la bergamote	6
Au citron	6
A l'estragon	6
A la fleur d'orange	6
Au jasmin	6
A la rose	6
A la tubéreuse	6
A la vanille	6
Parfumé	7

SIROPS DE VINAIGRES.

La Bouteille.

De vinaigre	6
Au citron	7
A la fleur d'orange	7
A la framboise	7
Au limon	7
A la rose	7
Agréable	7
A la vanille	9

MOUTARDES.

Le Pot.

En porcelaine	6
Avec armes	9
Aux trois armes	15
A l'ail	1 25
Aux anchois	1 25
Aux câpres	1 25
Aux câpres et anchois par extrait d'herbes fines	1 25
A la capucine	1 25
A la ciboulette	1 25
Au citron	1 25
De conserve	1 25
Aux cornichons	1 25
A l'échalotte	1 25
A l'estragon	1 25
Aux herbes fines	1 25
Au jus de citron	1 25
A la ravigote	1 25
De santé	1 25
Des six graines	1 25
A la choisi	1 50
A la maréchale	1 50
Aux mille feuilles	1 50
Aux morilles	1 50
Aux mousserons	1 50
Noire	1 50
Rouge	1 50
Suave	1 50
A la tomataise	1 50
Des 4 graines, pour les engelures, avec la poudre	1 75
Verte aux fines herbes	2
Aux truffes	2 50
En poudre, la livre	6

Elle se débite aussi par demi-livre et par quarteron.

FRUITS CONFITS AU VINAIGRE.

Le Bocal.

Ail mariné	2 50
Choux-fleurs à l'Angl.	2 50
Cornichons	2 50
Echalottes	2 50
Groseilles à maquereau	2 50
Haricots à la génoise	2 50
Noix à l'écossaise	2 50
Passe-pierre	2 50
Petits oignons	2 50
Bigarreaux	5
Graines de capucine	5
Melons marinés à l'anglaise	5
Piment	5
Poivrons confits à la façon de Turin	5
Abricots verts	3 50
Brugnons	3 50
Champignons	3 50
Epine-vinette	3 50
Pêches	3 50
Prunes	3 50
Blé de Turquie	3 50
Câpres	4 50
Achar indien	6
Pot-pourri	6
Truffes marinées	9

Tous les Vinaigres énoncés ci-dessus peuvent se transporter par mer, sans aucune crainte qu'ils se corrompent, à quelqu'éloignement qu'on les envoie. Plus ils se gardent, meilleurs ils deviennent. L'emballage est sûr.

MAILLE est le seul qui a le secret du véritable Vinaigre Romain, et de la Poudre de Tartre de Vinaigre, dont la vertu est si connue pour la bouche, inventé par MAILLE au mois de janvier 1752, et approuvé par le premier Médecin, sur l'examen que la Commission

The readers of the newspaper were the bourgeoisie and intellectuals, always interested in innovations and fond of life's comforts. These affluent customers were regularly informed of new varieties of vinegar created by La Maison Maille.

From 1752, Antoine-Claude also had the idea of offering to deliver his products, which he advertised in a notice published in the *Mercure de France*. To show what was available, he subsequently created a catalogue displaying his whole range of products.

This remarkable sense of innovation and communication guaranteed the reputation and success of La Maison Maille, which opened a store in 1760 at Sèvres, strategically positioned on the road to Versailles. The royal road was clear ahead.

The royal road

After years of creativity, it was not long before those in power started to take notice. In 1760, La Maison Maille became the official supplier to the Royal Court of Austria. Antoine-Claude Maille was then authorised to include the coat of arms of the Emperor of Austria and Queen of Hungary on his products. But the ultimate recognition came in 1769 when he was chosen by Louis XV to be official distiller and vinegar-maker to the king. His title of *vinaigrier-distillateur ordinaire* meant that he would supply the court every day rather than just on special occasions as was the case previously. He succeeded Le Comte who had recently died. Maille was already well known to the Court because Madame de Pompadour, chief mistress to Louis XV, was also a loyal client. With a residence on rue Saint-André-des-Arts, it was easy for her to purchase vinegar from her neighbour, or at least to have it delivered. The glamourous marquise used 37 different types of vinegar to maintain her beauty. However, there was one she purposefully avoided: the *Vinaigre à la Reine*, named in honour of Louis XV's wife, Marie Leszczynska. In fact, this *vinaigre de toilette* had been created specifically for the Queen, her rival.

In 1771, Antoine-Claude Maille extended his influence when he was granted the title of distiller and vinegar-maker to Empress Catherine II of Russia. In fact, like his father in Marseilles 50 years earlier, he took the initiative of sending as much vinegar as was required to stop the plague epidemic in Moscow, completely free-of-charge. Each successive generation of the Maille family seemed to inherit this capacity for philanthropy and political shrewdness.

La Maison Maille continued to prosper and then, in 1789, Antoine-Claude Maille went into partnership with André-Arnoult Aclocque, Commander General of the Parisian Guard and former brewer. In 1800, old and sick, he sold his business to Aclocque prior to his death in 1804. It was not until 1819 that the Maille family regained control of the business, this time by Robert, grandson of the founder who partnered with Aclocque's son when he came of age. The latter sold his share of the business in 1826, while Robert Maille entered into a new partnership with a certain Robillard. After the end of the 18th century, Maille vinegar and mustard was being sold all across Northern and Eastern Europe. This is supported by an article by Grimod de la Reynière, father of the food critic and creator of the famous *Almanach des gourmands*. In 1805, he wrote about mustard that '...the Northern peoples especially are so partial to it that a jar that costs 25 pennies in Paris will fetch up to 5 or 6 francs on the shores of the Baltic. The Russians, Danes and Swedes consume it in prodigious quantities: they eat it on bread as if it were jam.' (ref: *Almanach de Gourmands*, second year, 1805, p.96).

Throughout the 19th century, Maille continued to supply the great courts of Europe. Robert Maille was named vinegar-maker to King Charles X in 1829.

'Regimes came and went while Maille remained prominent with an increasingly large international presence.'

On left: Mustard dispensed by pump, "mustard on tap".
Double page spread following: Maison Maille, Dijon, 32, rue de la Liberté.

THE MAILLE COAT OF ARMS

Archives proving the authenticity of La Maison Maille titles have been found at the Bibliothèque Sainte-Geneviève in Paris. A register dating from the 18th century as well as articles from the periodical *L'Année Littéraire* (1767) and advertising in the magazine *Mercure de France* (from 1770) recount this first episode of the Maille story. To reward the talents of 'Sieur Maille' and the unrivalled quality of his products, Louis XV awarded him the title of *Vinaigrier-Distillateur Ordinaire* in 1769. In this capacity, he became official vinegar supplier to the King of France and was therefore allowed to associate the King's coat of arms to his own house. The tradition of these decorative symbols was subsequently retained, a symbol of the company's royal heritage and longevity over the centuries. Today, the historic coat of arms of La Maison Maille is iconic. In black and gold colouring, it depicts two angels holding and framing the royal mantle which itself features traditional emblems of sovereign power: three fleurs de lys, a laurel wreath and a cross of the Order of the Holy Spirit. The powerful and conquering monarchy is also represented by a crown on top of a fleur de lys which reigns over the coat of arms. The two characters are standing on a listel, a frieze bearing the famous rhyming slogan: *'Il n'y a que Maille qui m'aille'* (roughly translated as 'Maille mustard is my mustard').

Moutarde de MAILLE
Vinaigrier de L.L.M.M.
...eine d'Angleterre
...t les Empereurs
...riche et de Russie
à Paris

MAILLE
DEPUIS 1747

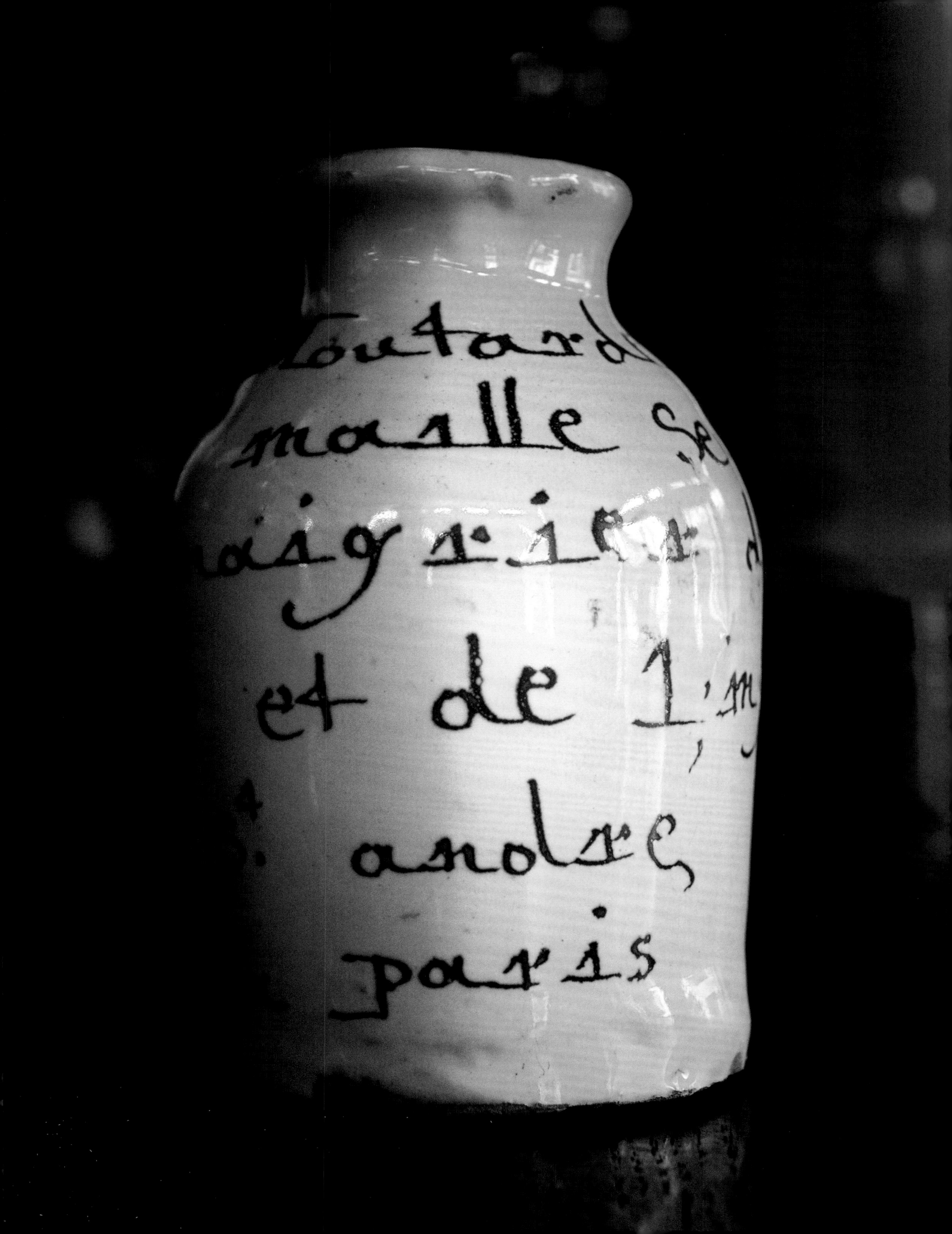
maille
et de
paris

In the following year, the King of England added La Maison Maille to his list of preferred suppliers. A few years later was the first *entente cordiale* initiated by Louis-Philippe and Queen Victoria. In the Second Empire, with Napoleon III favouring Bordin for political reasons, Maille extended his influence outside France and became official supplier to the major courts in Europe.

This century was the age of the industrial revolution with its grand world's fairs starting in 1851. In Europe and the United States, each participating nation showcased its technical and artistic advances. Maille regularly distinguished itself in these competitions by winning silver medals in Paris in 1867, 1878 and 1889, in Amsterdam in 1883 and in Antwerp in 1889.

WHAT IS
'DIJON MUSTARD'?

The appellation 'Dijon mustard' refers to a manufacturing process and is not a protected food name. It is used to describe mustard pastes made from brown or black mustard seeds. The mustard seeds are mixed with water, vinegar and salt, crushed and their tegument (mustard seed coat) removed. The final product must comprise at least 22% dry extract from mustard seeds (product remaining once the water has been removed) and no more than 2% tegument. It does not have to be manufactured in Dijon or from seeds harvested in Burgundy to be labelled 'Dijon mustard', and the manufacturing quality can vary greatly from one mustard to another. Maille mustard stands out from many other mustards with its unique creamy-smooth texture.

MAISON FONDÉE EN 1747

Rue Violet, 50

PARIS - GRENELLE

MOUTARDE

MAILLE

VINAIGRIER · DISTILLATEUR

V. TANDEAU Suc.

A new era for La Maison Maille

The 20th century started full of promise at a time when mass consumption was growing. Mustard and vinegar were on almost everyone's tables by this time. But then the First World War started and abruptly put a stop to La Maison Maille's rapid rise and international ambitions.

By the end of the war, Maille's business activities had been reduced to its grocery shops in Paris and in about a dozen other countries, including England and Denmark. Jean Herbout joined Maille in 1930. He breathed new life into the brand and became the architect of its renewal.

Il n'y a que Maille qui m'aille

As early as 1925, advertising slogans were all the rage. The best advertising for a brand was to be on everyone's lips. In 1931, Jean Herbout broached the subject with Emile Baudé, who was Maille's director at the time. In a relatively short amount of time, the two came up with 'Il n'y a que Maille qui m'aille', but were not entirely satisfied. However, they did eventually adopt it and could barely have imagined then that the slogan would be on everyone's lips more than 80 years later.

As for what we now call 'product packaging', there was a lot of work to be done. Jean Herbout looked to history and Maille's founding principles to create the labels, the coat of arms and pots. He designed pots identical to older versions with labels of black and gold, displaying the Maille coat of arms and printed with old lettering.

At the beginning of the 1930s, La Maison Maille modernised its production methods. At the same time, it decided to expand into new territories to increase visibility and accessibility. So it increased its presence in meat shops, a promising retail network that could be exploited due to meat's affiliation with mustard.

The brand also set about associating itself with luxury Parisian hotels and restaurants in 1934. It used a Trojan horse approach, where small elegant baskets filled with mustards and vinegars were placed on the capital's most fashionable tables. This was its first foray into the high-end market where it was to remain permanently a few decades later.

In the meantime, Maille had to defend its territory in the capital against the challenge from Amora. This competitor, created in 1919, went on the offensive with an advertising campaign in cinemas and on the bridges of Paris. Maille retaliated immediately by deploying its name in gold letters on the capital's roofs.

In 15 decisive years, Jean Herbout had managed to cure La Maison Maille of the malaise caused by World War I and had firmly returned it to its rightful place at the top table.

Refined tastes

In the 1960s, Maille was developing new recipes known as much for their creativity as their excellent quality.

It all started with Maille's gherkins. Until then, gherkins had been preserved in large amounts of vinegar and salt, which often imparted too much sourness for consumers. After 1952, the newly discovered process of pasteurisation was used for storing foods. This meant gherkins could be pickled with a sweeter flavour and crunchier texture. At the same time, Maille worked on a more subtle flavouring, using a tarragon base. Firm with just enough spiciness, Maille's extra-fine gherkins were a big hit.

As for mustard, it too became increasingly gourmet as more and more refined recipes appeared. In the 1970s, customers were being treated to special mustards made with green pepper, tarragon and shallots. These regionally inspired recipes were presented in beautiful containers, such as a whisky glass specially created by Cristal d'Arques. Another 18th-century inspired stoneware pot was used for traditional and fine mustard.

Its cork stopper and wire cap were reminiscent of a champagne cork. Glass jars then became even more elegant with the 'Fleur de Lys' jar, which included a metal screw cap.

Regarding vinegar, a premium range was launched in glass bottles, with flavourings such as tarragon, lemon and shallots. The 'prestige' range was introduced in 1979 with three exceptional vintages: an aged Bordeaux wine vinegar, a sherry vinegar and a raspberry vinegar. These exquisite flavours and decorative containers captured the imagination and provoked fascination just as they did in the royal courts centuries earlier. La Maison Maille was once again enjoying a premium reputation and its illustrious history was to continue being written.

International expansion

After the 1950s, Maille expanded into some 40 countries and had a significant presence in a dozen of them, including Canada, Germany, Great Britain, Australia, Brazil, Greece, Scandinavia and Japan. Three decades later, it became the most exported condiments brand in France. In 1983, it was present in 80 countries.

'Since 2003, drawing inspiration from many sources, Maille has been designing two annual collections of three seasonally themed mustards for its boutiques.'

La Maison Maille had become a global ambassador of French gastronomy and quality. But despite these French roots, local tastes were embraced and special flavours were created for these foreign markets, complementing the local cuisine while respecting culinary traditions. This global expansion was particularly driven by distributors who were very enthusiastic about promoting the quality of Maille in their respective countries. In the United States, Maille's expertise was recognised by the American Award 1987, a prize awarded by a jury consisting of US importers, food writers and personalities from the business world. And all the while the brand's reputation was being enhanced by country-specific marketing campaigns. In 1990, Maille's first international TV advert was broadcast on screens in Canada, and in the following year the slogan 'I did it Maille way' was filed, inspired by the song *My way* by Frank Sinatra — quite the endorsement.

Creative renewal

In more recent decades, La Maison Maille has regained its original creative momentum while staying faithful to the brand's roots: French gastronomy par excellence.

In the 1990s, Maille developed new original recipes that redefined the condiments market. Certain mustards and vinegars, which symbolise the know-how and creativity of Maille, were introduced in this decade, such as the Mustard Veloutée, Mustard with Honey, Balsamic Vinegar and the Mustard Fins Gourmets, the latter having been created for the 250th anniversary of Maille. Other recipes, such as the Wholegrain Mustard, were reworked to enhance aromatic qualities and texture. Since 2003, drawing inspiration from many sources, Maille has been designing two annual collections of three seasonally themed mustards for its boutiques. Developed in partnership with renowned chefs, these special collections are available exclusively from Maille boutiques.

In 2013, in the wake of this creative renewal and driven by enthusiasm for its products around the world, La Maison Maille took the step of opening boutiques internationally. The first overseas boutique, with an authentic French flavour, opened in London in October of the same year. It is to be followed by New York and other leading capitals on five continents over the coming years.

Right: Mustard on tap, Maison Maille, London, 2 Piccadilly Arcade.

Three Centuries of History

When La Maison Maille was founded in 1747, Louis XV was
King of France. It had not been around very long before France
went through the upheavals of the French Revolution. Because
André-Arnoult Aclocque, a partner in the Maille business, had
served as a guard for King Louis XVI on 10 August 1792, the
day when the Tuileries Palace was captured, Maille lost its royal
privileges in 1799 and was not a supplier for Bonaparte when
he declared himself First Consul. This did not prevent Maille from
pursuing its goals in the 19th century, which was a very unstable
time politically. Regimes came and went while Maille remained
prominent with an increasingly large international presence.
In the middle of the 19th century, Maille transitioned from
traditional artisan techniques to industrialised manufacturing
methods. The brand's expansion accelerated up until the
First World War when the economy was dealt a massive blow.
Barely two decades later came the Second World War.
Although weakened, the house of Maille survived these two
dark periods in history before going through a renaissance
of its own in the 1950s.

QUE MAILLE QUI M'AILLE

Maille: more than a mere brand

After having survived several centuries without disappearing and having faced huge food-culture revolutions while staying true to its values, these days Maille is a jewel in the crown among France's brands. Is there a French family that has not enjoyed Maille mustard with their meal at some point over the years? Are there many who have not crunched into a Maille gherkin with a nice slice of the best country ham? Who in France has not heard or said to themselves the famous words 'Il n'y a que Maille qui m'aille'? La Maison Maille is part of France's culinary history and remains a symbol of French food and culture to this day.

An iconic brand spanning three centuries

France's culinary heritage has a rich history going back many centuries. It is renowned for its refinement, diversity, quality of its products and an expertise that is passed on from generation to generation to protect this culinary excellence. Inscribed in UNESCO's Intangible Cultural Heritage list since 2010, French gastronomy does not rest on its laurels. It continues to innovate, reinvent itself and stand out as unique, reflected by the hundreds of award-winning chefs found in France. Maille is one of the most prominent and dynamic symbols of this gastronomic heritage as it has always been able to find fertile new ground for refreshing its image.

Since its very first days, Maille has been winning over the public and attracting attention with its never-ending pursuit of quality and innovation. Antoine-Claude Maille the younger was a born creator who exponentially increased the range of Maille vinegars on offer, for both the bathroom and kitchen. The times he lived in, the 18th century, was a golden age for condiments and French tables were some of the most refined in wealthy circles. In the 19th century, Grimod de la Reynière regularly showered praise on the creativity of Antoine-Claude Maille in his *Almanach des gourmands*, even going as far as claiming that 'the most inventive genius of mustard making is Sir Antoine-Claude Maille'. In 1808, he paid him and his rival Bordin the greatest of compliments by calling them the 'Corneille and Racine of mustard', two of the greatest French dramatists of the 17th century, which was somewhat akin to comparing them to Shakespeare and Marlowe.

Made in France

Although it has continued to evolve over the centuries and kept up with technical advances, Maille mustard making and vinegar making has always been French. Mustard was first made in Paris, handcrafted for over a century. Production then intensified from 1850

Opposite: Coat of arms designed by Jean Herbout in 1931.
Double page spread following: Maison Maille, interiors Dijon boutique.

HERITAGES DU TERROIR

Production Secrets

Maille's mustard-making process is unique. It involves principles that have barely changed since the business started: how the mustard seeds are selected, careful attention to texture and colour, characteristics of the ingredients and how they are chosen. Although the exact details are secret, we can reveal the main steps. First of all, the seeds are carefully sorted so only the best quality brown seeds are retained. Then comes the most delicate step which is to moisten the seed so the coat can be removed without the seeds popping. This is a Maille proprietary process and produces the unique taste. The seeds are then cracked without being crushed. They then resemble a yellow paste with traces of tegument remaining. This paste is then mixed with juice to create a texture similar to mustard in a jar. The next step is to sieve the paste very gently in order to refine it and to obtain a good creamy texture. Air is then extracted in order to prolong the shelf life as much as possible. Finally, the mustard is packed quickly in order to retain the freshness.

following the invention of a machine that could grind, crush and sift at the same time. At that time, the Maille factory was located on Rue Violet in the 15th arrondissement. In 1965, production was permanently relocated to Longvic near Dijon, where it remains today. Burgundian at heart, this was home for La Maison Maille.

As for vinegar, its fermentation process was shrouded in mystery until the second half of the 19th century. No one could explain what alchemy was behind the process of alcohol turning into vinegar. It took Pasteur and his discovery in 1865 of the bacterium responsible for this fermentation for the secret to be revealed. With this new scientific knowledge, vinegar making became more efficient and went through a long series of technological developments. Like mustard, Maille wine and cider vinegars are today produced in the Chevigny factory. An ageing cellar sits at the heart of this plant where hundreds of oak vats work their magic on vinegar for twelve months. Like wine, time is all-important and maturation in oak barrels allows its aromatic qualities to develop.

THE VARIOUS SPECIES OF MUSTARD PLANT

Mustard is a herbaceous plant. There are about 40 varieties around the world. The four main varieties are white mustard, wild mustard, brown mustard and black mustard. In France, a 1937 decree only allows the use of brown and black mustard, except for Alsatian mustard, which is made from white mustard. According to this decree, 'mustard is the result of the product obtained by grinding, optionally followed by sieving or sifting, seeds of black mustard or brown mustard or a blend of the two varieties.'

The most prestigious Maille vinegars age in this way, taking their time to develop their smooth and subtle fruity characters until they reach full maturity.

In 2015, spurred on by the success of its mustard served from the pump, La Maison Maille created two new vinegars to be served fresh over the counter. These two new products, called La Grande Reserve du Roy in homage to the illustrious history of the brand, are available in specially designed stoneware bottles that feature one of the brand's first labels. The Bordeaux Red Wine Vinegar and Sauternes White Wine Vinegar are now part of the range of gourmet and exclusive products found in Maille boutiques.

A symbol of French food and culture

Maille is one of the leading brands in the exclusive club of major French fine-food establishments and therefore represents a unique culture in the world.

The mustard of kings in the 18th century, Maille is now the mustard of connoisseurs. More than just a slogan, 'Il n'y a que Maille qui m'aille' is a motto and almost a profession of faith. Even outside France, the brand is proudly embraced by fine-food lovers who appreciate the variety and subtlety of Maille products.

Like other major luxury brands, Maille is a gourmet brand whose customers have refined tastes and a love of quality food. The coat of arms and royal crowns that decorate the black and gold labels are not just for decoration. They tell the story of the house of Maille by referencing its illustrious customers and show that it is no ordinary brand.

Maille boutiques, along with their atmosphere, the service and the excellence of their products, epitomise this unique *art de vivre*. These boutiques are the only place where connoisseurs can enjoy fresh mustard served from the pump and the inimitable flavours of this freshness. In all Maille boutiques, mustard served from the pump in stoneware jars is an elegant touch that pays homage to the master mustard-makers of the 18th century.

Opposite: New grey stone vinegar bottle filled at La Maison Maille (2015).

For several generations already, Dijon's residents have been able to visit the store on Rue de la Liberté to stock up on fresh Dijon mustard served from the pump. In the 1990s, the range of mustards on offer expanded to include Dijon Mustard with White Wine and Wholegrain Mustard with Chardonnay Wine. A decade later, Mustard with Speculoos and Chocolate, then Mustard with Chablis White Wine and Black Truffles and, more recently, Two Mustards with Sauternes White Wine were added to the range for the winter holiday season. Acclaimed for its exquisite and rare flavours, the Mustard with Black Truffles has become a Christmas classic with its ability to enhance dishes and delight guests during this season of enjoying the finest of foods. As the holiday season approaches, it is not uncommon to see queues of food-lovers at the boutique waiting for their turn at the pump.

These Maille boutiques have become such popular attractions because they offer the chance for connoisseurs from all over the world to soak up this refinement and experience a unique food culture. Some are local, others have crossed the Atlantic or arrived from Asia, but all have made a pilgrimage to La Maison Maille with their empty stoneware pots to fill them once again with fresh mustard. This is a wonderful testament to the excellence of the products as well as Maille itself, whose influence is now international.

From Tokyo and Montreal to Sydney and London, a stoneware pot of Maille mustard is always an elegant gift that fine-food lovers will appreciate. These same stoneware pots can be found on the tables of the world's best restaurants for diners craving authentic Dijon mustard.

Moreover, Maille boutiques are genuine creative workshops that develop a select range of mustards and vinegars with innovative and original flavours. These seasonal collections, which showcase the ingenuity of renowned chefs, are designed twice annually on a set theme. These creative collections ensure the boutiques remain dynamic and fresh, similar to fashion brands that change their lines with the seasons. As for the flavours, they surprise and delight the gourmets who look forward to these biannual events and the promise of new taste sensations. Luxurious and delicious, Maille seasonal collections are a very popular gift for a dinner invitation in any country. They are also a wonderful souvenir to take home after a trip to the home of gastronomy.

In Place de la Madeleine in Paris, Maille's founder constantly watches over his house from the wall where his portrait sits. The picture was bought in an auction by one of the current managers of La Maison Maille. The brand's history is to be cherished and preserved.

Maille enters the world's kitchens

After experiencing the splendour of the Royal Courts of the 19th century, La Maison Maille suffered the economic fallout of the two World Wars. During these hard times, mustard, gherkins and vinegar were not considered necessities, for obvious reasons. It was not until the 1950s that the brand began to spread its wings again. It travelled the world and success followed almost immediately. In just a few years, Maille had established itself in the United States, Canada, South Africa and Spain, and then in Australia and Japan in 1968. The list of countries continued to grow in the early seventies until Maille became the most exported condiments brand in France in 1983.

Thirty years later, Maille's market is impressive: it is a part of life for hundreds of millions of food-lovers across 80 countries and is maintaining its position as one of the largest French fine-food brands.

An international flavour

From England and Japan to Australia and Argentina, every national cuisine has its own traditional flavours and food culture. To fit into these diverse culinary landscapes, Maille had to develop a range of products specific to each country. Although the expertise remains French and the flavour subtleties bear the Maille signature, the recipes created are very much in line with local traditions.

For example, in Germany, Maille has developed its own Mittelscharf recipe, a medium mustard with very typical German flavours. Dijonnaise, a mayonnaise enhanced with Dijon mustard and mustard brans, has been a great success, especially in the United States because it balances the spiciness of mustard with the creaminess of mayonnaise, a combination that Americans are particularly fond of. The largest range of Maille mustards and vinegars is sold in Canada. Canada has been a home for the brand for 50 years now and was one of the first to launch Mustard with Honey onto its market, a unique recipe that marries the spiciness of mustard and the sweetness of honey. Maille gherkins have also been a spectacular success internationally for many years thanks to their uniqueness. The ones eaten in France are small, zesty and very crunchy. These are the qualities that have made them such a big hit outside France.

Because there is no substitute for tasting the actual product, Maille regularly organises events and cookery workshops in the world's major cities so that people can discover new flavours and gain some hands-on experience. Famous chefs man the stoves, designing creative recipes from Maille products and taking inspiration from them to give classic national dishes a new twist. This is how the Japanese — who love their condiments, especially rare and premium products — discovered the pleasures of mustard melted in a little soy sauce as an accompaniment to their famous sashimi and nigiri. As for the English,

they have become partial to reducing red fruit vinegar and pouring it over a cherry and almond pie.

This success is down to the work of many people, but especially Maille's distributors, who are true ambassadors of Maille and France in their countries. Over the years and even decades for some, they have cultivated partnerships with chefs and restaurants, and helped raise awareness of Maille products and their symbolism of French culture at events across the world. From New York and Melbourne to Montreal and Berlin, these distributors personify the passion at the heart of La Maison Maille.

After decades of gracing dining tables around the world, Maille is now a part of daily life in many countries. So much so that Maille mustard pots appear in many films and television series as essential components of a good meal. When Meryl Streep serves a sandwich to her ex-husband in the movie *It's Complicated*, she seasons it copiously with Maille mustard. When Julie Delpy welcomes her larger-than-life family to her New York apartment in *2 Days in New York*, a Maille mustard pot is on the table. And it is Maille once again that spices up *Modern Family* meals in the hugely popular US sitcom. Nor has its fame eluded global mega stars such as Madonna, who reportedly asked for Maille Wholegrain Mustard at a concert in Istanbul.

Another sign that there are very few places untouched by Maille is that a Maille mustard pot is often found in the most unlikely of places: a restaurant table on Easter Island and Stromboli; a small grocery store on the island of Santorini; a steak house in Durban, South Africa; and even more amazing, a jar of Maille mustard carried by porters on the steep slopes of Machu Picchu. It is undoubtedly a very famous condiment.

In order to maintain and strengthen ties with all these countries, La Maison Maille started opening boutiques in many capital cities in 2013. They are not just a showcase for Maille products, but also for creative and flourishing French cuisine.

Opposite: Unique Chandelier draws its design from replica mustard pots:
La Maison Maille, Paris, Carrousel du Louvre, opened in 2015.

Maille boutiques, windows into a unique *savoir-faire*

With such illustrious neighbours as Fauchon, Hédiard, Mariage Frères and Ladurée, Maille's boutique in Place de la Madeleine in Paris, which opened in 1996, is located in its rightful place among the elite of fine-food stores. Every customer is welcomed as an honoured guest and invited to experience a taste of traditional splendour among the warm decor, much like its predecessor in Dijon founded in 1845. Once within a Maille boutique, visitors are not just stocking up on mustard, vinegar and pickles, they come to discover an important part of French food culture. In October 2013, Maille opened its first boutique outside France with a new shop in London. As with the Dijon and Paris stores, the range of products on offer is exclusive to these boutiques. After London, a boutique opened in New York and others will soon come to other leading capitals across five continents. The London store is located in Piccadilly. This bustling street with its chic fashion brands has long been one of London's most prestigious areas and synonymous with elegance, luxury and tradition — the perfect location for a Maille boutique.

Upon entering the Maille boutique in Piccadilly Arcade, visitors are treated to a unique experience. Designed around a mustard organ concept, customers can explore a wide range of luxurious and refined products with help from knowledgeable guides who introduce the signature Maille flavours and its latest creations. From mustard with black truffles or

Above: La Maison Maille, NYC, 185 Columbus Avenue.

Above: Since 1996, La Maison Maille, Paris, 6 place de la Madeleine.

raspberry, to a velvety citrus vinegar and Dijon crème de cassis vinegar, there is a world of taste and texture sensations to discover. Each boutique is designed to showcase French gastronomy. Visitors are taken on a journey full of creativity, refinement and tradition. The Maille Boutique at Piccadilly Arcade is also the location of prestigious events organised by English chefs in collaboration with the boutique's mustard sommelier. The first-floor rooms are frequently used for organised tastings in partnership with the capital's top hotels and restaurants.

With boutiques opening in similarly prestigious locations around the world, more gourmets on every continent will soon be introduced to the ever-growing range of original and quality products from La Maison Maille.

CONTINUING THE TRADITION OF CREATIVITY AND BOLDNESS

From its very early days, La Maison Maille became a leading fine-food establishment due to the excellence of its products. Today, its mustards and vinegars are still appreciated by refined palates owing to their ability to offer a unique taste experience. They now form the foundation of marinades and sauces that take meats, vegetables, fish and shellfish to another level, not to mention some of the most audacious and inventive desserts.

Recognised for its creativity and experimentation, La Maison Maille offers new culinary perspectives to chefs and gourmets the world over. Whereas 1970s trends were rooted in tradition and products inspired by local flavours, the 1990s looked to outside influences for inspiration. This was when recipes with distinctive flavours such as Honey Mustard, Horseradish Mustard, and Mango Vinegar appeared. They are still some of the brand's bestsellers today. A new step was taken at the turn of the next millennium.

Seasonal collections

To 2003 and cooking had become a huge craze. Recipe books were bookshop bestsellers, cooking shows and magazines were everywhere, and chefs had become global celebrities. Inventiveness in the kitchen knew no bounds, previously unknown spices and ingredients had become must-haves and everyone was reaching for them to introduce new flavours to their cooking. The phenomenon was huge and pushed the limits.

As for Maille, the craze did not pass it by. On the contrary, the brand created quite a stir. Because gastronomy is seasonal, just like fashion, Maille's management decided to launch two collections per year. In the same vein as the major French fashion brands,

Maille was to now live in rhythm with spring-summer and autumn-winter, imparting seasonal colour and flavour to its creations.

For the first time, flavours were made from more than one ingredient, unlike the mustards created previously. All were gourmet and highly innovative with regard to ingredients. Collections were created from fresh cheeses, herbs and even flower petals. Certain recipes were subtle yet distinctive, made from Colombo spices, Espelette pepper and ginger, while others included valuable ingredients, such as Chablis and truffles. One was even developed from King Louis XV's favourite ingredients: Morello cherries, peas and even fennel, which was introduced to the Royal Court at the request of Catherine de Médicis, who apparently loved it. Despite the diverse range of ingredients, a common theme was that each collection included innovative flavour combinations that took consumers on a journey away from traditional recipes.

The idea was a huge success and the French were quick to embrace these new products. Consumers fell in love with the new flavours, which showed them how fun it was to be adventurous with classic condiments. After all, who could resist duck breast with candied orange peel and ginger mustard, or a lamb shank with hazelnut and black trumpet mushroom mustard? How about a mango-caramel tart with mango vinegar? And the potential for new discoveries is

Previous pages: La Maison Maille, London, 2 Piccadilly Arcade, opened in 2013. First boutique abroad.

endless — a feeling shared by many top chefs who can sense that the only limits are their own imaginations when using Maille mustards and vinegars.

In 2008, the concept of two-ingredient flavours was extended to limited-edition mustards served from the pump in boutiques. Some are now offered year-round, others are created specifically for the new-year celebrations and are only available during the holiday period. The flagship mustard in 2008 was a chocolate-speculoos flavour created for Christmas and available for two years. In 2010, it was a mustard with Chablis and pieces of black truffle, a particularly complex mustard with the black truffle coming through in both flavour and texture due to the inclusion of small crunchy pieces. Upon opening the pot, there is a glorious scent of truffles and tasting the mustard is an equally sublime experience. The effect is particularly striking when paired with a rich red meat. The success of this mustard was such that it has become a classic and is now available every year in boutiques during truffle season.

Since 2003, the most iconic seasonal collection flavours have stayed beyond their season and have now become part of the permanent vinegar and mustard range. Around 40 mustard and 20 vinegar flavours are now available year-round in Maille boutiques.

So what goes on behind the scenes? Before they are available for consumers to enjoy, these innovative mustard and vinegar flavours have to go through rigorous development and tasting. Although on paper it is relatively easy to think up new flavour combinations and to put forward increasingly appetizing ideas, implementation is decidedly more complex. It requires in the region of six to twelve months of work from the first flavour concept to launch of a mustard or vinegar. It all starts with a theme, a trend or a colour. Ideas are collected and approximately 25 flavours are retained. They are then developed by chefs from carefully selected fresh products. These products then go through a process of testing, improvement and repeated tastings until three of them stand out for being the most interesting, the most innovative and the most current in terms of cooking trends. A few months later, they represent the latest collection from La Maison Maille.

Spreading the word

In his time, Antoine-Claude Maille knew the importance of words for exposing his creations and tempting new customers. 'The public is informed...' he would say. Nearly three centuries later and after several revolutions in communication methods, advertising now plays a fundamental role in the products' success.

Since the 1930s, Maille has played on visual motifs of France's history and symbols of royalty. More than 80 years after its creation, the coat of arms with its royal emblems carries such visual impact and symbolism that the brand seems to have a timeless quality. The slogan has also passed into posterity.

During the post-war period and into the 1970s, Maille mainly focused on its production process to enter new markets, while advertising became a secondary objective. Everything changed in the 1980s when Maille invested heavily in advertising, like many other businesses. With mustard, the brand set out to conquer the condiment world via screens and magazine pages. Characters in the adverts were borrowed from French history. André Chénier and Chateaubriand, famous writers from the 18th century, featured in adverts about the history of France. Other campaigns showed the French aristocracy claiming that Maille mustard was a part of its heritage. In the 1990s, the communication kept the elite references but focused more on the product. From this period, one particular advert for olive oil stands out: the gold letters of Maille melt into liquid gold, which transforms into an olive as it is cast in a mould. Once this olive is pressed, it becomes a sublimely coloured olive oil. The whole sequence references the alchemy of yesteryear. The image is sophisticated, the music velvety: Maille shows itself as the quintessence of *savoir-faire*.

The 2000s were the golden age of Epicurean indulgence. The imagery portrayed was one of a refined art of living

Opposite: La Maison Maille, Paris, 6, place de la Madeleine, interiors.

in a world of connoisseurs. TV adverts were brimming with elegance and sensuality as other-worldly products seduced consumers. The eye of the camera would approach a product with desire, revealing it bit by bit and lingering on velvety textures, thus sending viewers into sensory overload. The temptation was irresistible, the pleasure palpable.

In 2014, a new campaign was launched to focus on the special moments shared from sitting down to eat with friends and family. Rather than dwell on Maille's glorious past, the campaign sought to affirm what it is today: free, creative and inspired. Gone are the references to characters of yesteryear and well-to-do families with outdated language; the brand's unique expertise is for everyone's enjoyment. Maille is always at our tables and a part of our meals, our laughter, our memories and unforgettable shared moments. At the center of thousands of conversations across multiple generations, it represents the heart and soul of the dining table.

At the top chefs' table

Since 2003 and the launch of its seasonal collections, Maille has gained a new reputation for haute cuisine. With its unique range of flavours, award-winning chefs are increasingly embracing Maille products in search of gastronomic perfection. In the never-ending pursuit of innovation and new flavour combinations, they are acknowledging the potential that mustard and vinegar holds. And not only do these products pose a creative challenge, but also a fun one, as illustrated by Hélène Darroze's capon with truffle mustard, or a saffron mustard marinade for a carpaccio of scallops on a bed of radishes, as proposed by Christophe Moret, Head Chef of Lasserre restaurant. And then there is scrambled eggs with truffle mustard by Philippe Renard, Head Chef of Lutetia, and a strawberry sorbet with Burgundy raspberry cream mustard by Eric Briffat, Head Chef of Hotel Georges V. Vinegar too has inspired prestigious chefs, such as a cocktail made from vodka and mango vinegar

created by Potel & Chabot and served at the opening of the London boutique. The lucky diners who get the chance to taste these delicacies experience something truly rare and exquisite. Furthermore, every season a top chef is invited to become an ambassador for Maille and to create recipes from the current seasonal collection. Emmanuel Renaut, a *meilleur ouvrier de France* and Head Chef of the three-starred fine dining restaurant Flocons de sel in Megève, is the 2014 ambassador.

London-based and Michelin-starred French Chef Bruno Loubet is behind Maille's 2015 recipe collection. He has reinvented classic British cuisine with Maille products, including Rhubarb and Strawberry Savoury Mustard Muffins with Comté Cheese.

Maille mustards and vinegars have become a constant source of inspiration for chefs and it is not uncommon for chefs to visit the boutique on Place de la Madeleine to stock up on supplies to feed their creativity — especially those who want to push the limits, break the rules and take gastronomy to new heights. Maille has the credentials to be a partner of choice for these chefs as its products are able to add that special something to innovative dishes. Its glorious past will always be part of the brand, but it now prefers to look forward, to break new ground. Maille's expertise and boldness have won the favour of the most creative culinary minds, who in turn have found in Maille a source of inspiration and fun in their pursuit of invention.

In family kitchens

Although these chef's creations represent the pinnacle of gourmet eating, the fact remains that these fine-dining experiences are not the daily reality of ordinary food-lovers. Small homemade dishes are by far the more common part of meal times than haute-cuisine by Michelin-starred chefs. Therefore, what better reason is there to make daily meals a delicious experience every time? And when friends are visiting, the food served up can be just as fun as

the atmosphere in the dining room. However, quality ingredients are essential to impress those around the table and that includes the indispensable condiments that complement any dish. Not everyone has the time to find Colombo spices to season curries, or ginger to balance a sauce, or Thai spices to add kick to a red meat, or chanterelles and oyster mushrooms to add character to game; so Maille's range of flavours is more than worth the quick trip to the local shop where the equal of these ingredients are within easy reach. Maille vinegars, pickles and mustards are always on hand when those everyday meals need to feel that bit more special. When a cook needs to invent, surprise, enhance or bring out any flavour, Maille products are an obvious choice. It only takes a drop of mustard or a few splashes of vinegar to create something special from something ordinary.

This is the philosophy that has inspired Maille from the beginning and is continued by Jean-Pierre Biffi with the recipes he has specially designed for this book. He invites everyone to put this theory into practice and to start a culinary journey of discovery with Tuna-tomato muffins, sundried tomato glaze (p.84), Mussels soup with saffron mustard (p.142), and Backed pineapple with Caribbean Juice with mango vinegar (p.156). Maille mustards, vinegars and pickles are ready to guide each cook — professional or amateur, novice or experienced, creative or classic — to gastronomic excellence.

There is no better advice to those who strive to reach new heights with their cooking than to choose their mustard with great care. Because, as with a good wine, pairing a mustard with a dish is an art, the results of which will provoke strong feelings of joy, satisfaction and wonderment in anyone lucky enough to experience it.

After more than 265 years in existence, Maille has become a household name that has retained its original verve and inventiveness. With generations of talented individuals within its ranks and now celebrated on all continents, it is a success story of how a family's vision can delight millions of people around the world. As a symbol of French food and culture, Maille is proud of its history and region of origin, and excited to share its unique art de vivre with others. Like the great French explorers of previous centuries, Maille set off to find new markets with no guarantees of success. But with the same boldness found in its products and an enduring appetite for discovery, it conquered these new markets by embracing international tastes and cultures.

In a truly global world, Maille has looked to these foreign countries as both a source of inspiration and as an opportunity for introducing its traditions to new consumers. For Maille, cooking is an art, one that needs a new canvas for every season. Gourmets, Epicureans, the curious, connoisseurs and the world's top chefs all appreciate the brand's innovations as ingredients for their own creative ideas. Maille contributes to redefining the rules of dining, to pushing the boundaries. It is constantly asking new questions of what food can be and in this way it adds spice and flavour to everyone's lives. It tirelessly seeks to reinvent itself, to challenge itself, to embrace diversity, to absorb influences, to be on the cutting edge and to set new trends. And this is down to the boldness behind its creations and which inspires the inventive minds of award-winning chefs.

Refined, elegant, unique, yet remaining accessible to all. Such quality is no longer just for the elite, but now transcends all social constructs.

After a rich and eventful history, full of political and economic upheaval, La Maison Maille has now discovered its DNA, the creative intensity that flows through its veins. It is now as self-assured as ever.

While it was known as lavish and sometimes too exclusive in past generations, it has matured and opened up to all. It is now chic, creative and in line with current trends. But that is not to be confused with trendy, which is often ephemeral; instead, it is timeless, with an endless capacity to evolve. And because food and dining always has and will always be one of life's great pleasures, its future is as bright as ever.

GOURMET
RECIPES

Between Friends

Truffled Soft-Boiled Quail Eggs
in Vermicelli Nests
– 71 –

Vitello Served in Little Gem Lettuce Cups,
Parmesan Mustard
– 75 –

Cream of Cranberry Beans with Tomato Vinegar
– 76 –

Sardine Rillettes with Dijon Mustard
– 81 –

Mackerels with Lemon-Harissa Mustard, in a Jar
– 81 –

Vegetables Marinated in Balsamic Vinegar
– 83 –

Tuna-Tomato Muffins, Sundried
Tomato Glaze
– 84 –

Smoked Salmon Paris-Brest with
Dill and Lime Mustard
– 87 –

Artichoke Risotto with Garlic-Lemon Mustard
– 88 –

Winter Vegetable Millefeuille
– 91 –

Veal Piccata alla Zingara
– 92 –

Gingerbread Ice Cream with and Gingerbread
and Chesnut-Honey Mustard
– 95 –

Truffled Soft-Boiled Quail Eggs
in Vermicelli Nests

Makes 12

Preparation time: 30 minutes
Resting time: 3 hours

Ingredients

12 fresh quail eggs

1 1/4 cups (300 ml)
Maille chardonnay white
wine vinegar with white
grape juice

1 1/4 cups (300 ml)
truffle juice

3 1/2 oz (100 g)
rice vermicelli

4 1/2 cups (1 litre)
sunflower oil

1 3/4 oz (50 g) Maille
Chablis and black truffle
mustard

Salt and pepper

Boil some water in a saucepan and gently drop in the
quail eggs. Cook for 2 1/2 minutes, then drain the eggs
and cool them in a large bowl of iced water for 5 minutes.
Drain the eggs and transfer them to another bowl. Add
the white wine vinegar and let sit for 2 hours, which will
have the effect of dissolving the shells. Peel the eggs gently.

Put them in a bowl with the truffle juice and marinate
for 1 hour.

Heat the sunflower oil to 350 °F (180 °C, gas mark 6) in
a large pot and deep-fry the rice vermicelli, turning them
over regularly for a few minutes.

Drain the vermicelli, divide the mass into small cups,
shaping them into small nests. Season with salt and
pepper. Drain the quail eggs, put one into each nest and
serve with Chablis and black truffle mustard on the side
as a seasoning.

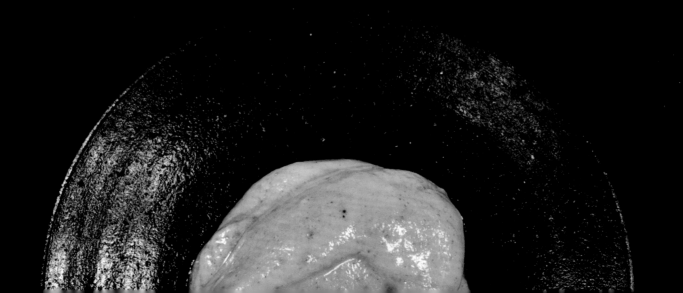

Vitello Served in Little Gem Lettuce Cups

Parmesan Mustard

Serves 6

Preparation time: 30 minutes
Cooking time: about 1 hour

Ingredients

17 oz (500 g) veal fillet or loin

3 tbsp olive oil

2 little gem lettuces

1 tbsp (20 g) Maille parmesan cheese
and basil mustard

1/4 cup (25 g) freshly grated parmesan

Fleur de sel

Freshly ground black pepper

Preheat oven to 140 °F (60 °C, gas mark 2). Season the piece of veal with salt and pepper. Sear it on all sides in a very hot pan on high heat with a little olive oil. When the meat is lightly coloured, wrap it in a sheet of greaseproof paper and put it on a baking sheet.

Bake for 1 hour. The meat should still be pink inside. You may check the inner temperature with a meat thermometer; the meat should not be warmer than 133 °F (56 °C) at the centre. Let cool and refrigerate.

Trim the little gem lettuces and tear off the leaves to use them as small dishes.

When the veal has cooled, slice it very thinly. Season it with the remaining olive oil and a little fleur de sel.

Spoon the mustard into a piping bag fitted with a smooth nozzle. Drop a dot of mustard in the hollowest part of each lettuce leaf. Add the sliced veal on top and garnish with a pinch of grated parmesan.

Cream of Cranberry Beans
with Tomato Vinegar

Serves 4
Soaking time: 12 hours
Preparation time: 15 minutes
Cooking time: 1 hour

Ingredients

9 oz (250 g) dried haricot beans, cranberry or white

1 onion studded with 2 cloves

2 cloves garlic, peeled

1 carrot, peeled

1 bouquet garni
(thyme, bay leaf, parsley)

4 tbsp crème fraîche

5 tbsp Maille blend of vinegar and tomato purée

4 thin slices of Serrano cured ham (optional)

Salt and pepper

Put the beans in a large bowl, cover with cold water and let soak overnight. The next day, drain them and transfer them to a large saucepan.

Add the onion (studded with the cloves), garlic, carrot and bouquet garni. Cover with 6 1/3 cups (1.5 litres) of water and bring slowly to a boil.

Lower the heat and simmer, covered, for 1 hour. Remove the bouquet garni. Strain the beans and vegetables, setting aside the cooking liquid. Purée the beans in a blender, adding enough cooking liquid to get a smooth consistency. Stir in the crème fraîche and 4 tbsp of tomato vinegar, then season with salt and pepper.

Divide the cream of beans in soup plates or bowls and decorate the surface with small dots of the remaining tomato vinegar.

Preheat your oven to 212 °F (100 °C, gas mark 3-4).
As an extra garnish, you may add a few Serrano ham chips — just bake the chips in a 350 °F (170 °C) oven for 10 minutes between two sheets of greaseproof paper sandwiched between two baking sheets.

Maille Dijon Originale

ecipe for Dijon mustard invented by Antoine-Claude Maille
remains the reference today. But over time,
he selection of mustard seeds, rigorous quality controls
Maille's own manufacturing process has improved it further.
Its subtle spiciness, translucent yellow colour,
ure and exceptional lifespan are the result of unique expertise.
It is ideal in vinaigrettes and paired with red meats.
This Dijon mustard's subtle notes make it perfect
for richly flavoured dishes.

Sardine Rillettes with Dijon Mustard

Serves 6

Preparation time: 45 minutes

Ingredients

8 3/4 oz (250 g) canned sardines

1/4 cup (50 g) lightly salted butter, softened

2/3 cup (150 g) Saint-Môret® cheese or cream cheese

Juice of 1/2 lemon

1 tbsp Maille Dijon mustard

6 pieces of Melba toast (see page 130)

Salt and pepper

Drain the sardines and mash them with a fork in a salad bowl. Stir in the softened butter and cream cheese. Add the lemon juice and Dijon mustard. Season with salt and pepper. Mix well.

Spoon the sardine rillettes into a glass jar and keep refrigerated. Serve with Melba toast on the side.

Mackerels with Lemon-Harissa Mustard, in a Jar

Serves 6

Preparation time: 25 minutes
Cooking time: 10 minutes

Ingredients

12 oz (350 g) fresh mackerels

1 sachet of dried court-bouillon

1 bunch chives

3 1/2 oz (100 g) crème fraîche

3 1/2 tbsp (70 g) Maille lemon and harissa spices mustard

6 pieces of Melba toast (see page 130)

Salt and pepper

Gut the mackerels, clean them and cut off their heads. Rinse them well. Dissolve the dried court-bouillon in 3 1/8 cups (750 ml) of water and bring to a boil. Turn off the heat, immediately drop the mackerels in the water and let sit for about 10 minutes. Drain the fish and let cool.

Split each mackerel in half, remove all bones and finely shred the flesh with a fork in a salad bowl. Wash the chives, pat them dry and slice them finely. Add to the shredded mackerel with the crème fraîche and mustard. Season with salt and pepper to taste. Mix well and spoon into a glass jar. Refrigerate.

Serve cold, with Melba toast.

Vegetables Marinated
in Balsamic Vinegar

Serves 6

Preparation time: 20 minutes

Marinade: 24 hours

Ingredients

9 oz (260 g) carrots

4 baby courgettes

3 baby ears of sweet corn

2 oz (60 g) girolle mushrooms
(or any other seasonal
mushroom) ·

1/4 cup (50 g) sugar

3 tbsp Maille white balsamic
condiment

Peel the carrots and cut them into long sticks, about the length of a 1-pint jar. Wash the courgettes and cut them into sticks of about the same length, without peeling them. Rinse the corn and pat it dry.

Put all these vegetables into the jar, arranging them according to colour.

Put the sugar into a bowl and cover with 1/2 cup (100 ml) of very hot water. Stir to mix, add the condiment and mix well. Let sit for 5 minutes, then pour this marinade over the vegetables. Shut the jar tightly and tie a length of raffia around the top with a small label to identify the contents.

These marinated vegetables should be refrigerated; they'll keep for one week, but you can eat them the day after they are made.

Tuna–Tomato Muffins,

Sundried Tomato Glaze

Serves 8

Preparation time: 30 minutes
Cooking time: 20 minutes

Ingredients

2 1/2 lb (1.18 kg) flour

25 g baking powder

1 cup (160 g) freshly grated parmesan

4 tbsp olive oil

5 1/2 oz (160 ml) milk

6 very large eggs (60 g each)

5 1/2 oz (160 g) sundried tomatoes

10 1/2 oz (300 g) tuna belly preserved in a glass jar (in water)

1/4 cup (60 g) butter

1 egg white

1 tbsp Maille Sherry vinegar with sundried tomatoes

1 3/4 cups (230 g) confectioner's sugar

1 lime

In a large bowl, mix the flour, baking powder and grated parmesan. Make a well in the centre, pour in the olive oil and milk, mix gently and gradually, then stir in the eggs one by one.

When the batter is smooth, add the finely chopped sundried tomatoes and the finely diced drained tuna.

Preheat oven to 325 °F (170 °C, gas mark 5-6). Butter 8 muffin tins (or brioche moulds, or small pudding moulds). Divide the batter between the tins and bake for about 20 minutes.

Meanwhile, make the glaze: pour the raw egg white through a fine sieve into a bowl, then add the sherry vinegar with sundried tomato.
Mix well, then stir in half the icing sugar.
Whisk well, then stir in the remaining icing sugar until you get a smooth glaze.

Wash and dry the lime; grate its zest finely.

When the muffins are ready, take them out of the oven and unmould them. Thoroughly brush their entire top surface with the glaze, then decorate with the grated lime zest.

Smoked Salmon Paris–Brest
with Dill and Lime Mustard

Serves 6

Preparation time:
40 minutes
Cooking time: 30 minutes

Ingredients

1/3 cup (55 g) butter

3/4 cup (90 g) flour

3 eggs

1 head of root celery

1 lemon

2 cups (500 ml) milk

7/8 cup (200 g) heavy cream

3 tbsp (60 g) Maille dill and lime mustard

12 oz (340 g) smoked salmon, sliced

3 tbsp olive oil

1 tbsp balsamic vinegar of Modena

3 oz (80 g) mesclun (mixed salad greens)

3/4 oz (20 g) fish eggs

A few sprigs of dill

Salt and pepper

Make a choux pastry: in a saucepan, pour 7/8 cup (200 ml) water, add 1/3 cup (55 g) diced butter, a little salt and bring to a boil. When the water boils, add all the flour at once and immediately stir vigorously with a spatula until the dough leaves the side of the pan. When that happens, take off the heat and stir in the eggs one by one. Mix thoroughly.

Preheat oven to 350 °F (180 °C, gas mark 6, fan position). Lightly butter a baking sheet. Spoon out some small balls of dough, or push them out of a piping bag and lay them side to side. Bake for 35 minutes, take the pastry out of the oven and let it cool completely.

Make a celery purée: peel the root celery, rubbing it with a little lemon juice to keep it from discolouring, then cut it into pieces and put in a saucepan. Add the milk and 4 1/2 cups (1 litre) of water. Season with salt and simmer for about 30 minutes. Meanwhile, whisk the heavy cream to firm peaks. Carefully drain the root celery and purée in a food mill. Stir in the whipped cream and dill and lime mustard. Let cool completely.

Roll up the slices of smoked salmon, wrapping them very tightly in cling film. Cut the rolls in 3/8 in (1-cm) chunks, then gently peel off the film and sprinkle the salmon chunks with the remaining lemon juice.

Make a vinaigrette with the olive oil, balsamic vinegar, salt and pepper. Season the mesclun salad with the vinaigrette.

Cut the choux puffs horizontally in two and fill them with celery purée, then put the caps back on. Dot each chou with a little celery purée, then place a small roll of salmon on top. Decorate with fish eggs. Arrange the seasoned mesclun. Garnish with small dill sprigs.

Artichoke Risotto
with Lemon and Garlic Mustard

Serves 6
Preparation time: 30 minutes
Cooking time: 15 minutes

Ingredients
6 large round artichokes
2 onions
2 tbsp olive oil
5 tbsp (100 g) Maille lemon and garlic mustard
7/8 cup (200 g) heavy cream
1 leaf bear's garlic
1/2 cup (100 g) freshly grated parmesan
1/2 cup (100 g) finely grated Gruyère cheese
Salt and pepper

Cut off the stalks from the artichokes, pull out the leaves, discard the hard, fibrous parts and the choke, keeping only the tender flesh. Set the hearts aside. Collect the leaves and the stalks in a large saucepan, season with salt and pepper, and add water just to cover. Bring to a boil, take off the heat, cover the pan and let steep for 30 minutes. Strain the liquid and set aside. Discard the stalks and leaves.

During the steeping time, chop the artichoke hearts in tiny, regular-shaped dice. Peel the onions and slice them thinly.

Heat the oil in a heavy pan on medium heat. Add the onions and fry until they are translucent, about 2 to 3 minutes. Add the diced artichokes and pour in the reserved cooking liquid to barely cover the ingredients. Cook for 3 minutes, then stir in the mustard and cream. Bring to a boil before adding the finely chopped bear's garlic leaf. Taste and correct seasoning and keep warm.

Preheat oven to 325 °F (170 °C, gas mark 5-6). Make the parmesan tuiles: mix the parmesan and Gruyère cheese, line a baking sheet with greaseproof paper, drop disks of mixed grated cheeses on the paper and bake for 5 minutes until golden-brown. Take the tuiles out of the oven and let cool, then peel them off the paper delicately.

Serve the artichoke risotto with its sauce in soup plates or bowls. Garnish with the cheese tuiles.

Winter Vegetable Millefeuille

Serves 6

Preparation time: 1 1/2 hours
Cooking time: 1 hour

Ingredients

2 pre-rolled disks of puff pastry
2 1/4 lb (1 kg) Jerusalem artichokes
1 1/8 lb (500 g) parsnips
1 chicken stock cube
1 kg kuri squash (potimarron)
2 tbsp honey
6 Belgian endives
3 tbsp (40 g) butter
1 tbsp (20 g) Maille
blue cheese mustard
1 tbsp (20 g) Maille walnut mustard
Salt and pepper

If you are using frozen puff pastry, defrost it for 1 1/2 hours at room temperature. Peel the Jerusalem artichokes and the parsnips. Crumble the stock cube in a saucepan containing 6 1/2 cups (1.5 litres) of water. Add the peeled vegetables, season with salt and pepper, bring to a boil and simmer for 30 minutes. Drain the vegetables (keeping the cooking broth) and slice them thinly.

Boil down the cooking broth on high heat in the uncovered pan until syrupy (about 30 minutes).

Preheat oven to 300 °F (150 °C, gas mark 5). Peel the squash and cut the flesh in thin slivers, about 2 mm thick. Brush them with half the honey, arrange them on a sheet of greaseproof paper on a baking sheet and bake for 10 minutes. Set aside.

Trim the endives and halve them lengthwise. Cut off the bitter cone at the base of each endive, then cook them in a buttered heavy pan with the remaining honey for 30 minutes.

Preheat oven to 350 °F (180 °C, gas mark 6). Roll out the puff pastry, if necessary and cut out three disks, 24 cm in diameter. Lay them on a baking sheet, lay another baking sheet on top and bake for about 12 minutes until pastry is golden.

Divide the reduced broth between two bowls. Add the blue cheese mustard to one and the walnut mustard to the other. Mix well.

Lay one disk of puff pastry on a serving dish. Cover it with the braised endives and brush them with the walnut mustard broth. Place a second disk of puff pastry on top, then alternate the thin slices of parsnip and Jerusalem artichoke on it in a rosette pattern. Brush these with some blue cheese mustard broth. Finally, place the last disk of puff pastry on top of the vegetables and cover it with squash slivers in a flower shape.

Veal Piccata
alla Zingara

Serves 6
Preparation time: 45 minutes
Cooking time: 15 minutes

Ingredients
1.5 lb (720 g) veal filet mignon
1 shallot
7 oz (200 g) mushrooms
2 lemons
3 1/2 oz (100 g) Maille mini-gherkins
7 oz (200 g) cooked ham
20 g butter
5/8 cup (150 ml) dry white wine
2 1/4 oz (60 g) sundried tomatoes
1 1/4 oz (30 g) tomato sauce
6 sprigs tarragon
14 oz (400 g) conchiglioni rigati 126 pasta
(large fluted pasta shells)
2 tbsp olive oil
Flour
Salt and pepper

Cut the filet mignon into 24 regular-sized, 1/3 in (1-cm) thick slices. Season them with salt and pepper, flour them on both sides, shaking them to remove excess flour.

Peel the shallot and slice it finely. Trim the mushrooms, iscarding the sandy base of the foot, try not to wash them but wipe them with damp kitchen paper instead. Slice them finely and sprinkle them with lemon juice. Slice the gherkins and finely shred the ham.

Cook the pasta in plenty of boiling salted water for 11 minutes. Drain them carefully, put them in a large bowl, pour the olive oil over them and mix well. Keep warm.

Melt the butter in a large frying pan. When it is quite hot, lay the veal slices flat on its bottom and sear them for 2 to 3 minutes on each side. Remove them from the pan and keep warm.

In the same frying pan, sauté the finely sliced shallot for 2 minutes, then season with salt and add the white wine. Stir with a spatula to deglaze the juices, then boil down by half. Add the shredded sundried tomatoes, tomato sauce, chopped tarragon, gherkins, ham and mushrooms. Stir well and heat for a few minutes.

Divide the pasta between the plates, add the ham-and-mushroom zingara preparation on top, then place the veal slices on the side. Sprinkle with lemon juice and serve.

Gingerbread Ice Cream
with Gingerbread and Chesnut Honey Mustard

Serves 6

Preparation time: 15 minutes
Freezing time: 1 hour

Ingredients

1 quart (1 litre) vanilla
ice cream

3 1/2 oz (100 g) gingerbread

4 oz (120 g) Maille
gingerbread and chesnut
honey mustard

Take the ice cream out of the freezer to soften a little.
While it warms up, cut the gingerbread into small,
5/8 in (1.5-cm) cubes. Put the ice cream in a large bowl
and knead it with a spatula, adding first the mustard,
then the gingerbread. When the mixture is smooth,
freeze it again for 1 hour. Scoop the ice cream into
balls cut with an ice-cream scoop and serve. You may
serve thin, lightly toasted slices of hazelnut and raisin
bread on the side.

MAILLE et AC

...llateurs du Roi et de LL. M...

Rue Saint-André-des-Arcs, n.° 16, et...

...mposition générale de toutes sortes de V...
...et de toutes sortes de Vinaigres tant pou...

VINAIGRES

De Parfums et Aromatiques,

A l'usage des Bains et Toilettes, distillés au verre, et différens Vinaigres servant à des opérations chimiques.

	La Bouteille.
A l'absinthe	5f
A l'ail distillé	5
A l'angélique	5
Au basilic	5
Au baume franc	*5
Au cochléaria	5
Au coq	5
Distillé	5

VINAIGRES DES VISA...

De Parfums et Aro...

De délices.
Au passulat
Ambré
A l'américaine.
A la belle Éléonore.
A la créole.
A la duchesse
De Hongrie
A la maréchale.
Suave.
Des sultanes
Au benjoin
A la cannelle

Cocktails — grab your shaker

Mango Vodka Cocktail

Bloody Mary with Horseradish Mustard

Soft Cocktail with Red Fruits

- 98 -

Small Shrimp Skewers, Thai Style

- 101 -

Pink Maki

- 103 -

Foie Gras Bars with Cherries

- 107 -

Sea Bass Tartare with Rocket Jelly

- 111 -

Scallop Carpaccio with Beet Chips

- 113 -

Lobster Club Sandwich with Dijon
Blackcurrant Liqueur Mustard

- 114 -

Duck Magret in a Nougat Shell

- 118 -

Tarragon Turbot in Harlequin Dress

- 120 -

Raspberry Feuilleté

- 124 -

Cocktails
Grab your shaker

Mango Vodka Cocktail

Serves 1

1/10 oz (1 tbsp) Maille vinegar with mango purée
3/10 oz (3 tbsp) mandarin orange juice
3/10 oz (3 tbsp) mango nectar
3/10 oz (3 tbsp) vodka

Pour into a shaker the mango vinegar, mandarin orange juice, mango nectar and vodka. Shake vigorously, then pour the contents into a chilled cocktail glass, on ice if you wish.

Bloody Mary
with Horseradish Mustard

Serves 1

1/2 cup (120 ml) tomato juice
2 3/4 tbsp (40 ml) vodka (one shaker capful)
1 dash Tabasco
1 tsp Maille horseradish mustard
Celery salt

In a shaker, pour the tomato juice and vodka (as much as the shaker cap contains). Add the dash of Tabasco, a few pinches of celery salt and the horseradish mustard. Shake well and serve chilled.

Soft Cocktail
with Red Fruits

Serves 1

1 tbsp dried goji berries
3.5 oz (100 g) sugarcane syrup
1/10 oz (1 tbsp) Maille vinegar with red fruits
6/10 oz (6 tbsp) rasberry nectar
3/10 oz (3 tbsp) pear juice

Soak the goji berries in the sugarcane syrup until plump. Meanwhile, in a shaker, mix the red fruits vinegar, rasperry nectar and pear juice. Shake well. Drain the goji berries and put them in the glass. Pour the contents of the shaker over them and serve chilled.

Small Shrimp Skewers
Thai Style

Makes 12 skewers
Preparation time: 25 minutes
Marinade: 20 minutes

Ingredients
6 large raw shrimp, peeled
3 tbsp dry white wine
1 3/4 oz (50 g) Maille mango
and Thai spices mustard
1 3/4 oz (50 g) daikon
1 3/4 oz (50 g) black radish
1 3/4 oz (50 g) large pink radish
4 tbsp olive oil
2 limes
Espelette pepper, salt and
freshly ground black pepper

Using the tip of a knife, pull out the black vein that runs along the back of each shrimp. Rinse the shrimp, then boil them for 45 seconds in a saucepan of water with the white wine. Drain the shrimp and halve them lengthwise.

Put the shrimp in a bowl, add the mustard and mix well to coat them entirely. Set aside.

Peel the daikon, black radish and pink radish and slice them thinly in order to get 12 thin slices of each.

In a deep dish, mix the oil, the juice and grated zest of a lime, a little salt, black pepper and Espelette pepper. Add the radish slices and marinate for 20 minutes, then drain.

Using small wooden or bamboo skewers, stick 1/2 mustard shrimp and 1 slice of radish on each one. Just before serving, sprinkle the shrimp skewers with the finely grated zest of the second lime.

Pink Maki

Serves 6

Preparation time: 30 minutes
Cooking time: 15 minutes
Refrigerating time: 2 hours

Ingredients

4 1/4 oz (120 g) sushi rice

1 tsp rice spirit, e.g. sake

1 tbsp rice vinegar

1 tbsp Maille glaze citrus vinegar

2 tsp sugar

1 oz (30 g) candied ginger

2 1/2 oz (70 g) pink grapefruit segments

1 rose (organically grown)

Salt and pepper

Rinse the rice in several changes of water. Drain carefully, then cook it in boiling water or steam it for 15 minutes. Pour it in a deep dish.

In a bowl, mix the rice spirit, rice vinegar, citrus vinegar and sugar. Season with salt and pepper. Pour this preparation on the cooked rice and mix thoroughly.

Finely chop the candied ginger and finely dice the grapefruit segments. Mix them into the seasoned rice.

Lay a large sheet of cling film on your work surface. Lay the rice on it and roll it tightly in the film into a cylinder. Refrigerate for 2 hours.

Pluck out the rose petals and chop them into thin slivers. Take the rice roll out of the refrigerator, peel off the film, roll the rice cylinder in the chopped rose petals and cut it into 1 1/4 in (3-cm) slices.

Foie Gras Bars
with Cherries

Serves 6

Preparation time: 30 minutes
Cooking time: 5 minutes

Ingredients

12 3/4 oz (360 g) semi-cooked (*mi-cuit*) duck foie gras

7 3/4 oz (220 g) sour cherry purée

1 tsp Maille red fruit vinegar

2/3 cup (15 g) agar-agar

16 fresh cherries

1 loaf of brioche bread

1/4 cup (50 g) butter

Salt and pepper

Cut the foie gras into 6 rectangular bars, 3 1/2 in (9-cm) long and 1 in (2.5-cm) wide. Lay them side by side on a nonstick baking sheet, spacing them so they do not touch.

Pour the cherry purée in a saucepan. Add the vinegar, mix and bring to a boil. Add the agar-agar and boil for 10 minutes, whisking constantly. Take off the heat.

Pour this syrupy jelly over the foie gras bars, then refrigerate.

Wash the cherries, pat dry, remove their stones and cut each cherry into two pieces. Cut 6 bars of the same size as the foie gras bars from the brioche bread. Fry them in a pan in the hot butter for 2 to 3 minutes, turning them over several times until golden.

On each serving plate, lay a bar of cherry-jelly-coated foie gras and a bar of fried brioche bread side by side. Decorate with the pieces of fresh cherries.

Red Wine Vinegar

MAILLE GRANDE CUVÉE

Maille's Grande Cuvée Red Wine Vinegar is the equivalent
of a great vintage wine in its field. Made from selected red wines,
grape juice is added to balance the acidity and to impart sweetness.
It is then aged 12 months in oak barrels, giving the flavours time
to develop nuance and subtlety. The finished product is exquisite
with a perfect balance between intensity and roundness.
In the kitchen, it is ideal for deglazing meat juices, blending with soy sauce
to give steamed vegetables a lift, or to add interest to an omelette.
It goes well with a myriad of other condiments and can form the body
of a sumptuous vinaigrette. The complexity of Maille's Grande Cuvée
Red Wine Vinegar makes it an elegant and essential
condiment in any kitchen.

Sea Bass Tartare
with Rocket Jelly

Serves 6

Preparation time: 45 minutes
Refrigerating time: 1 hour

Ingredients

1 1/4 lb (500 g) skinless and boneless sea bass fillets, diced

Juice and finely grated zest of 2 limes

4 tbsp Maille olive oil

1 tbsp (20 g) Maille basil mustard

1 fennel bulb

8 leaves gelatin

2 3/4 oz (75 g) rocket (arugula)

Espelette pepper

Salt and pepper

In a deep dish, mix the lime juice and finely grated zest, 2 tbsp olive oil, the basil mustard and 2 pinches of Espelette pepper. Add a little salt and the diced fish, cover and refrigerate for an hour.

Trim the fennel bulb and grate it, using a mandolin or a coarse grater. Set it aside in a bowl of cold water.

Soak the gelatin in a bowl of cold water for 5 minutes. Boil 1 2/3 cups (400 ml) salted water and blanch the rocket leaves in it for 30 seconds. Drain the leaves, squeeze them dry, then dissolve the drained leaves of gelatin in the blanching water. Mix well. Purée the leaves in a blender, then add the cooking water. Let cool; when the mixture becomes syrupy, pour it into a dish and refrigerate for 30 minutes until it sets into a jelly.

Using round cutters of different diameters, cut the jelly into disks and use them to decorate the plates, leaving enough space between them for the sea bass tartares. Spoon out the fish mixture onto the plates into round disks, pressing them slightly.

Drain the fennel and toss it with the remaining olive oil. Season with salt and pepper. Garnish the top of the sea bass tartares with the finely sliced fennel.

Serve with plain toasted bread.

Scallop Carpaccio
with Beet Chips

Serves 6

Preparation time: 1 hour
Cooking time: 5 minutes

Ingredients

2 raw red beets
1 1/4 cups (300 ml) peanut oil
1/4 cup (30 g) flour
12 scallops, shelled and cleaned
3/8 cup (100 ml) Maille olive oil
2 limes
1/2 head of root celery
1 egg yolk
1 tsp Maille mustard with celeriac
and block truffle
1 cup (250 ml) grapeseed oil
Salt and pepper

Peel and thinly slice the beets. Using a round 2 1/3 in (6-cm) cutter, cut these slices into neat disks. Heat the peanut oil to 280 °F (140 °C, gas mark 4-5) in a large, heavy-bottomed saucepan. Dip the beet slices in flour, shake them to remove excess flour, then deep-fry them for 5 minutes until very crispy. Drain on kitchen paper, season with salt and set aside.

Rinse the scallops and pat dry. Cut them horizontally in 1/16 in (2-mm) thick slices. Mix the olive oil with the lime juice and grated zest. Season with salt and pepper and set aside.

Peel the root celery and grate it coarsely. Make a mayonnaise: whisk the egg yolk with the mustard with with celeriac and block truffle, a pinch of salt and a little freshly ground black pepper. Pour the grape seed oil in a thin stream, whisking all the while, until the mayonnaise is thick. Then add the remaining oil in a steadier stream, still whisking. Mix the grated celery and the mayonnaise and refrigerate.

Brush both sides of the scallop slices several times with the olive oil-lime marinade.

Divide the seasoned celery between 6 plates (preferably black, for the colour contrast) in small portions. Cover them with scallop slices and decorate with fried beet chips.

Lobster Club Sandwich
with Dijon Blackcurrant Liqueur Mustard

Makes 6 sandwiches

Preparation time: 50 minutes
Cooking time: 12 minutes

Ingredients

1 lobster 1 1/2 oz (600 g)

1 egg yolk

3/8 cup (100 ml) grapeseed oil

2 tbsp classic vinaigrette
(made with olive oil
and lemon juice)

1 1/2 tbsp (30 g) Maille Dijon
blackcurrant liqueur mustard

2 tomatoes

2 carrots

3 oz (90 g) rocket (arugula)
leaves

12 slices of white bread

Salt and pepper

Remove the rubber bands from the lobster's claws, then drop the lobster in a large pan of salted boiling water, head first and tail folded up. Bring to a boil and count 12 minutes from that moment. Drain the lobster, throw it in a large pan of very cold water to interrupt cooking, then drain again and shell the lobster, picking out all the flesh and cutting the tail into thick slices. Season with salt and pepper and set aside.

Make a mayonnaise by whisking the egg yolk with the grapeseed oil, Dijon blackcurrant liqueur mustard and oil. Season with salt and pepper and refrigerate.

Wash the tomatoes, slice them thinly. Peel and grate the carrots and season them lightly with vinaigrette. Wash and dry the rocket. Toast the white bread.

Spread one side of the toasted bread with mayonnaise. Garnish half of the buttered toast with rocket, grated carrots, tomato slices and lobster. Cover with the remaining buttered toast and press lightly to seal each sandwich.

Tip: Large cooked and peeled shrimp can be used as a substitute for lobster.

See overleaf for recipe photo

Duck Magret
in a Nougat Shell

Serves 6

Preparation time: 20 minutes
Cooking time: 1 hour to 1 1/2 hours

Ingredients

3 1/3 cups (450 g) raw red beets

6 oranges

2 tbsp (40 g) Maille candied orange peel and ginger mustard

3 duck magrets

5 1/4 oz (150 g) soft nougat

2 tbsp Maille raspberry vinegar

Salt and pepper

Preheat oven to 350 °F (180 °C, gas mark 6). Wrap the beets in aluminium foil and bake them for 1 hour to 1 1/2 hours depending on their size. When the tip of a knife goes through a beet easily, they are cooked.

Meanwhile, make the sauce and prepare the magrets. Squeeze the juice from the oranges, pour it through a strainer into a saucepan. Boil it down on high heat until syrupy, then add the candied orange and ginger mustard. Keep warm.

Peel off the fatty skin from the magrets, then sear them in a nonstick pan for 5 minutes on each side. Transfer them to a plate, let them cool and halve each one of them lengthwise. Cut the soft nougat into 6 thin slivers, put one on each half-magret and bake in a 350 °F (180 °C) convection oven for 5 minutes.

Remove the beets from the foil, peel them and purée them in a blender, adding the raspberry vinegar.

Divide the sauce between the serving plates, stretching it into a line with the back of a spoon. Cover with a piece of magret and drop a quenelle of puréed beet on the side.

Tarragon Turbot
in Harlequin Dress

Serves 6

Preparation time: 30 minutes
Cooking time: 20 minutes

Ingredients

6 fillets of turbot, skinless and boneless, 5 1/2 oz (150 g) each

1 1/4 lb (500 g) red and white cherry tomatoes

1/2 bunch tarragon

1 1/4 cups (120 g) dried breadcrumbs

2 shallots

1 bay leaf

3/4 cup (230 g) Maille specialty mustard with tarragon

1/2 cup (120 ml) dry white wine

5/8 cup (150 ml) heavy cream

Salt and pepper

Lay the fillets in a baking dish. Season with salt and pepper.

Wash and dry the tomatoes. Slice them very thinly as if for a carpaccio. Remove the stalks from the tarragon and finely chop the leaves. Mix them with the breadcrumbs. Peel the shallots and finely slice them. Finely chop the bay leaf.

Brush the fillets of turbot with 1/2 cup (180 g) of tarragon specialty mustard. Cover with tomato slices, alternating colours so as to obtain a Harlequin-like colour pattern. Sprinkle with tarragon breadcrumbs.

Preheat oven to 340 °F (170 °C, gas mark 5-6).

Mix the white wine with an equal quantity of water and pour that around the fish. Add the shallots and bay leaf.

Bake for 20 minutes.

Drain the fish fillets, taking care not to break them and arrange them on a serving dish. Add the cream and remaining mustard to the cooking liquid and blend until smooth.
Taste and correct seasoning, then cover the fish fillets with this sauce and serve.

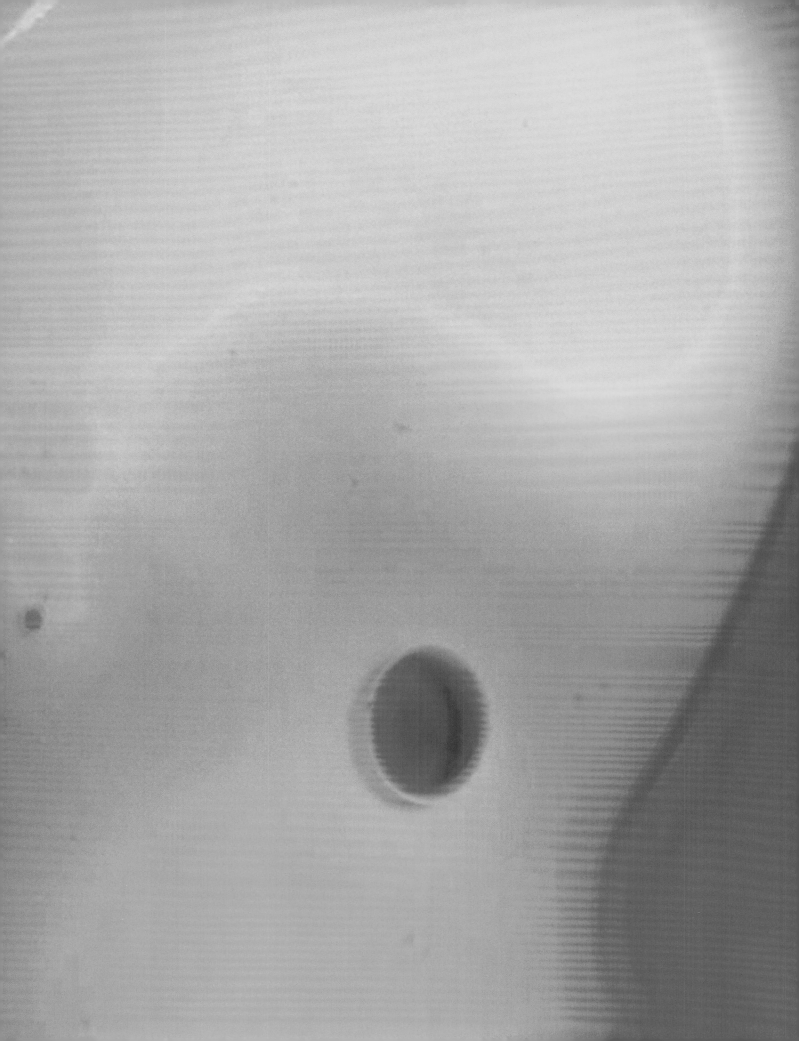

Raspberry Feuilleté

Serves 6
Preparation time: 30 minutes
Cooking time: 35 minutes

Ingredients
1 roll prepared puff pastry
(fresh or frozen)
4 1/4 cups (1 litre) milk
1 vanilla bean
4 egg yolks
1 cup (200 g) sugar
3/4 cup (100 g) sifted flour
7 tbsp (100 g) butter
6 tbsp Maille raspberry vinegar
1 tbsp grenadine syrup
4 cups (500 g) fresh raspberries
3/4 cup (100 g) pistachios,
shelled and skinned

Defrost the puff pastry if necessary and cut it into a 10 in (26-cm) disk. Set is aside, sandwiched between two baking sheets.

Make a pastry cream: bring the milk to the boil in a saucepan, adding the vanilla bean slit lengthwise.
Take off the heat and cover.

Put the egg yolks in a deep dish, beat them well and add the sugar. Whisk vigorously until thick and foamy. Add the sifted flour one spoonful at a time, then pour the boiling milk over the mixture (after having removed the vanilla bean), whisking well. Pour into a saucepan and cook on low heat, stirring all the while with a spatula, until boiling point. Add the diced butter a little at a time and mix well.

Preheat oven to 350 °F (180 °C, gas mark 6).
Bake the puff pastry until golden, about 12 minutes.
Take it out of the oven and let cool.

Pour the raspberry vinegar and grenadine syrup in a small saucepan and boil down on high heat until syrupy. Set aside and let cool.

Spoon the pastry cream into a piping bag. Pipe it onto the disk of puff pastry into large dots. Place one raspberry, hollow side up, on each dot, then pour the reduced vinegar syrup into each raspberry hole. Decorate with chopped pistachios.

Family Moments

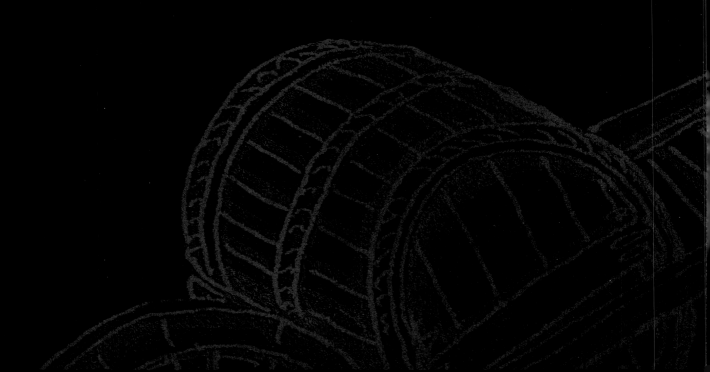

Melba Toast
with Mushrooms

Serves 6
Preparation time: 30 minutes
Cooking time: about 30 minutes

Ingredients
2 1/4 lb (1 kg) white button mushrooms
3 shallots
5 1/4 oz (150 g) butter
2 2/3 tbsp (70 g) Maille chablis
and black truffle mustard
6 large slices of
white sandwich bread
Fleur de sel
Salt and pepper

Make a mushroom duxelles by cleaning and trimming 1 3/4 lb (800 g) of the mushrooms, and cutting off the sandy base of the stalk. Wash the mushrooms quickly, pat them dry and chop them finely (heads and stalks). Peel and finely chop the shallots.

Melt 3 1/4 oz (90 g) of the butter in a large saucepan, add the shallots and cook on low heat, stirring, for 3 to 4 minutes. Add the mushrooms and cook on low heat, uncovered, stirring from time to time until all moisture has evaporated. Let cool, then transfer to a glass jar.

Cut off the crusts from the sandwich bread, then lay the slices flat on your work surface. Flatten them with a rolling pin and cut them into 1 1/2 x 5 in (4 x 12-cm) rectangular slices.

Preheat oven to 350 °F (180 °C, gas mark 6). Melt the remaining butter on low heat in a small saucepan, skim the foam on top. Brush both sides of the bread slices with this clarified butter and bake in the oven until golden.

Meanwhile, clean the remaining mushrooms (do not wash them; you can wipe them clean with damp kitchen paper) and finely slice their heads. Spread the mushroom duxelles onto the pieces of Melba toast and cover with slivers of raw mushroom. Add a pinch of fleur de sel and serve.

Maille Clips

Makes 12 clips

Preparation time: 35 minutes
No cooking required

Ingredients

1 large, long, brightly
coloured red carrot

3 1/2 oz (100 g) Comté
cheese, rind removed

2 1/2 oz (70 g) butter

40 Maille extra-fine
cornichons

Fleur de sel

Wash and trim the carrot, then pat it dry. Using a mandolin
or a coarse grater, cut 12 thin carrot strips, 4 in (10-cm) long.
Cut the Comté cheese into 12 thin square slices, 2 1/2
x 2 1/2 in (6 x 6-cm) and 1 1/6 in (1-mm) thick.

Using a spatula, work the butter until soft, adding a little
fleur de sel.

Drain the cornichons, cut 24 of them into thin matchsticks
and the remaining 24 into tiny dice. Mix the tiny dice
into the butter.

Lay the carrot slices vertically on your work surface, then
cover each slice with a Comté slice horizontally in a cross
shape. Add a small dab of soft butter and sprinkle with
some cornichons matchsticks. Fold the carrot slices over
the garnish and secure with a small clip.

Maille Cornichons

Nature's gifts require attention at every step of their development
if their true glory is to be revealed. With Maille's cornichons,
it all starts with harvesting. Once they have matured,
they must be harvested within about an hour. Maille's extra-fine
cornichons benefit from this art, which is why they are
the ideal size and have a perfect crunch. Aromatised with tarragon,
they have a balanced, pleasant flavour. No wonder that connoisseurs
can identify a Maille pickle from any other. Many would consider
a tomato sauce to be lacking without its subtle acidity and
likewise a plate of cold cuts without its curved silhouette on the side.
And when the aperitifs arrive, who can resist the satisfying crunch
of a Maille cornichon as an appetizer and perfect start to an
evening of good company and good food.

Croque-Monsieurs
Black and White

Makes 20 croques

Preparation time: 20 minutes
Cooking time: 12 minutes

Ingredients

5 large slices of white
sandwich bread

5 large slices of dark
buckwheat bread (same size
as the white bread)

2 1/2 tbsp (50 g) Maille
Dijon mustard

5 slices cooked ham

7 oz (200 g) Comté cheese,
without the rind

25 g butter

Spread all the slices of bread with the mustard.
Trim the ham to the exact size of the bread.
Cut the cheese into thin slices, then trim these
to the same size as above.

Lay one slice of white bread on the work surface.
Cover with a slice of ham, then with a slice of cheese,
then a slice of dark bread and repeat until all the
ingredients are used up. Press the top of the sandwich
so that all the layered ingredients adhere together.

Preheat oven to 340 °F (170 °C, gas mark 5-6). Lightly
butter your baking sheet and lay the sandwiches on it.
Bake for 12 minutes.

Let cool slightly, then cut each Maille croque-monsieur
into four square pieces. Alternate the black and white
surfaces in a checkerboard fashion then serve.

Maille Rich Country Dijon Mustard

Connoisseurs appreciate this mustard for its nuances of flavour
and texture. Created especially for the 250th anniversary
of La Maison Maille, the recipe was somewhat revolutionary
for its combination of mustard paste and whole grains.
This feature is typical of the creative boldness of Antoine-Claude Maille
who first invented this new type of mustard. There is instant pleasure
with the first bite as the whole grains burst in the mouth.
Then comes the complexity of flavour of this sophisticated recipe:
intense aromas and bright spices, pleasantly tempered
by a smooth creamy texture. This mustard works wonders
with red or white meats and provide a truly
different taste experience.

Sea Bream in Puff Pastry,

Tomato and Zucchini Tian

Serves 6

Preparation time: 30 minutes
Cooking time: 20 minutes

Ingredients

6 tomatoes

5 zucchini

1 garlic clove

6 skinless and boneless sea bream fillets,
5 oz (150 g) each

4 tbsp (80 g) Maille pesto and rocket
(arugula) mustard

2 disks of puff pastry,
about 10 1/2 in (26 cm) in diameter

2 crêpes

1 3/4 oz (50 g) dry breadcrumbs

2 egg yolks

Olive oil

Thyme

Salt and pepper

Wash and pat dry the tomatoes and courgettes.
Cut them into regular-sized slices. Preheat oven to 400 °F
(200 °C, gas mark 6-7). Peel the garlic clove and rub the inside
of a baking dish (or tian) with it. Alternate the slices of tomatoes
and courgettes in the dish in a tiled pattern. Season with salt
and pepper, sprinkle with thyme and add some olive oil in a thin
stream over the surface. Bake for 20 minutes.
Take the tian out of the oven, cover it and keep warm.

While the tian is baking, season the sea bream fillets with salt
and pepper, then brush them with pesto-rocket mustard.
Lay one crêpe on each disk of puff patry, sprinkle with half
the breadcrumbs. Lay the sea bream fillets in the middle.
Fold the sides of the crêpes over the fish, then bring both sides of
the puff pastry together, shaping it like a cockscomb and sealing
with egg yolk. Prick the pastry with a fork in several places.

Bake in a 350 °F oven (180 °C, gas mark 6) for about 15 minutes.
Put the tian back in the oven for a few moments so that it may
be served warm with the fish in puff pastry. Cut each puff pastry
parcel in three portions.

For children, you can make a fish shape out of the puff
pastry by drawing scales and a head with the tip of a knife
before baking.

Mussel Soup
with Saffron Mustard

Serves 4

Preparation time: 20 minutes
Cooking time: 30 minutes

Ingredients

4 1/2 cups (1 litre) mussels

1 lemon

3 garlic cloves

2 shallots

1 carrot

1 tbsp olive oil

7/8 cup (200 ml) dry white wine

5/8 cup (150 ml) crème fraîche

2 tbsp (40 g) Maille saffron and Isigny crème fraîche mustard

2 slices of slightly stale white bread

1 oz (25 g) butter

5 g saffron threads

Salt and pepper

Brush the mussels under cold running water until clean, pulling off the threads from the shells. Rinse the mussels in several changes of cold water, discarding any that remain open. Drain all the remaining mussels. Squeeze the juice of the lemon through a fine strainer.

Peel 2 of the garlic cloves, the shallots and the carrot. Chop the garlic and shallots, finely dice the carrot. Heat the oil on high heat in a large pan, add the garlic and shallots and sweat for 2 minutes while constantly stirring.

Add the mussels and the carrot, then the white wine and half the lemon juice. Cover and cook on high heat, stirring once or twice until all the mussels are open. Discard the ones that don't open. Drain all the others, leaving all the broth in the pan.

Pour 1 1/2 cups (350 ml) of water in the pan and boil down on high heat, uncovered, for about 10 minutes. Meanwhile, take half of the mussels out of their shells and leave the other half whole.

Mix the crème fraîche with the saffron mustard and stir this into the mussel broth. Taste and adjust seasoning with salt and pepper. Blend with a hand mixer while adding the remaining lemon juice. Keep warm.

Rub the bread slices with the last peeled garlic clove. Cut the bread into small dice and sauté them in a pan with the melted butter. When the croûtons are golden, drain them.

Divide the shelled mussels into four soup bowls or plates. Pour the hot soup over them. Garnish with the mussels still in their shells, the small croûtons and the saffron threads.

"Barbes de Capucin" Salad
with Black Olive Tuiles

Serves 6
Preparation time: 30 minutes
Resting time: 14 hours
Cooking time: 4 minutes

Ingredients
1 cup (150 g) pitted black olives
3 tbsp (40 g) butter
1/3 cup (35 g) flour
1 egg white
1 oz (30 g) glucose
3 bunches of barbe-de-capucin
(forced wild chicory, white dandelion
may be used instead)
3 tbsp (50 g) Maille whole grain
mustard with black olive
3 tbsp olive oil
1 tbsp Maille blend of vinegar
and tomato purée
1 1/3 cups (70 g) sundried tomatoes
Fleur de sel and pepper

Cut each olive in half, then squeeze all the olives with your hands to get rid of most of their moisture and oil. Spread them on a baking sheet and dry them overnight (about 12 hours) in a 175 °F oven (80 °C, gas mark 2-3).

Pulverize the dried black olives in a blender; you should obtain a powder as thin as fleur de sel. Dry it again in the oven, still at 175 °F (80 °C), while you continue with the preparation.

Beat the butter in a bowl until light and creamy.
Beat in the flour, a few pinches of fleur de sel and finally the egg white. Next beat in the black olive powder, making sure it is quite dry.
Heat the glucose after heating it in a ladle, then beat it into the mixture. Cover the batter and refrigerate for 2 hours.

Trim the barbe-de-capucin, wash it and drain it carefully, then chop it into pieces.

Make a vinaigrette by beating together the olive oil, the black olive mustard and the vinegar. Season with salt and pepper, then pour the vinaigrette into a salad bowl.

Preheat oven to 320 °F (160 °C, gas mark 5-6). Take the black olive batter out of the refrigerator and spoon out small quantities of it on a nonstick baking sheet, giving them a round shape and spacing them well. Bake for 4 minutes, then peel them off the baking sheet and let cool. While they are still hot, you can give them a curvaceous shape by laying them on a rolling pin, or shape them into thin tubes by wrapping them around the handle of a wooden spoon. Let dry.

Finely dice the sundried tomatoes.

Toss the barbe-de-capucin in the salad bowl with the vinaigrette, add the diced sundried tomatoes, then, at the last moment, the black olive tuiles.

Licorice Chicken on Skewers
Iranian Rice

Serves 6

Soaking time: 2 hours
Preparation time: 20 minutes
Cooking time: 25 minutes

Ingredients

3 1/2 oz (100 g) dried barberries,
sour cherries or goji berries

1 onion

4 1/2 oz (120 g) butter

1/2 cup (90 g) sugar

10 oz (300 g) basmati rice

1 3/4 lb (750 g) chicken aiguillette fillets

12 licorice sticks

1 jar of Maille mustard with honey
and balsamic vinegar of Modena

Salt and pepper

Put the barberries (or other dried berries) in a large bowl, cover them with water and let them soak for 2 hours. Drain.

Peel the onion and slice it thinly. Melt 3 1/2 oz (90 g) of butter on low heat in a large thick-bottomed pan; add the sugar and cook until lightly browned and caramelized. Add the sliced onion, then the rice and stir until each grain becomes translucent. Add the drained barberries and 3 1/2 cups (850 ml) water. Bring to a boil, lower the heat, cover and cook gently for 20 minutes.

While the rice is cooking, cut the chicken fillets into 24 thin strips, about 1 oz (30 g) each. Season them with salt and pepper. Halve the licorice sticks lengthwise. Use them as skewers and put the chicken strips on them in a wavy pattern. Brush them with 2 1/2 tbsp (40 g) of balsamic honey mustard. Heat the remaining butter in a large pan and sear the skewers for 7-8 minutes on each side.

When the rice is done, fluff it with a large two-pronged fork and transfer it to a serving dish, piling it up in the middle. Place the chicken skewers around the rice and serve with some honey mustard with balsamic vinegar of Modena on the side as a condiment.

Maille Honey Dijon Mustard

The beautiful warm colour of this mustard hints at its strong character.
And tasting it is like tasting no ordinary mustard. The secret
behind its Oriental notes lies with a very sophisticated recipe:
a subtle balance between mustard, honey, sugar and many spices.
Both round in body and full of spice, Mustard with Honey
enhances everything it touches. White meats, duck and filet mignon
take on hot and spicy nuances when paired with this mustard.
It is perfect for deglazing with a little vinegar and should also
be tried with crème fraiche, in vinaigrettes, marinades or as a little dip
for cheese. For the more adventurous, duck or poultry terrines
become truly gourmet when this mustard is incorporated.
With thousands of applications, this wonderfully
heady mustard is sure to delight.

Veal Shank Parmentier
with Dried Prunes in Armagnac Brandy

Serves 6
Preparation time: 20 minutes
Cooking time: 2 1/2 hours

Ingredients
1 whole veal shank 4 1/2 lb (2 kg)
1 onion
2 cloves
3 carrots
2 small leeks
1 hearts of celery
1 tsp black peppercorns
1 tsp coarse salt
1 bouquet garni
3 1/4 lb (1.5 kg) potatoes
1 lemon
1/2 cup (100 g) sugar
2 1/2 oz (70 g) dried prunes
8 3/4 oz (250 g) butter
3 tbsp (60 g) Maille Mustard with dried prunes and armagnac brandy
Salt and freshly ground pepper

Put the veal shank in a large pan and cover it with cold water. Bring to a boil, skimming regularly to remove all fat and impurities that rise to the surface. Peel the onion, then pierce it with the cloves.

Peel the carrots, trim the leeks and the celery hearts. Wash the vegetables, cut them into chunks and add them to the veal shank in the pan. Add the onion, bouquet garni, peppercorns and coarse salt. Cover the pan, keeping the lid slightly ajar, bring to a boil and simmer for 2 hours on low heat.

Peel and wash the potatoes, put them in a saucepan, cover with cold water and cook for 30 to 35 minutes. Cut the lemon into 4 quarters and boil it with the sugar in 2 cups (500 ml) water for 35 minutes.

Remove the stones from the dried prunes. Finely dice the flesh. Mash the potatoes by putting them through a potato ricer. Beat in the diced butter and the diced prunes. Drain the lemon, cut off the flesh and finely dice the peel. Add it to the mashed potatoes. Mix well and set aside.

When the veal shank is done, drain it, pick all the meat from the bones and shred it with two forks. Pour the cooking stock through a fine sieve, pour 4 1/2 cups (1 litre) into a saucepan and boil it down to 7/8 cup (200 ml). Mix the shredded meat with the reduced stock and the mustard with dried prunes and Armagnac brandy.

Preheat oven to 400 °F (200 °C, gas mark 6-7). Spread the meat on the bottom of a casserole dish and cover with the mashed potatoes. Smooth the surface and bake for 5 minutes. Serve hot.

Pasta Arancini
with Sun-dried Tomato and Espelette Chilli Mustard

Serves 6

Preparation time: 30 minutes
Resting time: 30 minutes
Cooking time: 20 minutes

Ingredients

15 leaves gelatin (2 g each)

4 1/2 cups (1 litre) heavy cream

14 oz (400 g) freshly grated parmesan

14 oz (400 g) coquillette pasta
(small macaroni pasta)

3 oz (80 g) grated cheese

2 tbsp (40 g) Maille sun-dried tomato and
Espelette chilli mustard

1/2 cup (70 g) flour

3 egg whites

3 1/2 oz (100 g) dry breadcrumbs

3 tbsp squid ink

4 1/2 cups (1 litre) peanut oil

Salt and pepper

Soak the gelatin in a large bowl of cold water.
Meanwhile, heat the cream on low heat in a saucepan,
then add the Parmesan. Mix well. Drain the gelatin,
squeeze dry and add to the cream. Mix again, pour into
a large bowl and set aside.

Boil some salted water in a large saucepan, add the
pasta and cook for 3 minutes. Drain, put them in a
casserole dish, add the grated cheese, sun-dried tomato
and Espelette chilli mustard. Stir in the parmesan cream.
Cover and refrigerate for 30 minutes.

Using a soup spoon, shape this preparation into
24 equal-sized balls.

Put the flour, slightly beaten egg whites and breadcrumbs
mixed with the squid ink in three different bowls.
Heat the peanut oil to 340 °F (170 °C) in a deep-fryer.

Roll the balls in the flour, then in the egg whites and
finally in the breadcrumbs. Coat them with egg white
again, then in breadcrumbs. Deep-fry them for 5 minutes
each batch.

Serve 4 hot arancini per person.

Baked Pineapple

with Carribean Juice

Serves 6

Preparation time: 30 minutes
Cooking time: 25 minutes

Ingredients

1 ripe pineapple

6 oz (170 g) pineapple pulp

3 oz (90 g) mango pulp

3/8 in (1-cm) piece of fresh ginger

3 vanilla pods

1/2 cup (100 g) sugar

2 tbsp Maille mango vinegar

Peel the pineapple and remove the eyes.
Keep refrigerated. Heat the two fruit pulps in a saucepan
on low heat. Add the peeled and finely diced ginger,
3 tablespoons water and the seeds from the vanilla pods
(slit the pods lengthwise then scrape them with the tip
of a knife to release the seeds. Keep the pods.)

Add the sugar to a thick-bottomed saucepan.
Cook it, without adding water or stirring, to 330 °F (165 °C),
until you get a light-coloured caramel. Pour the warm
fruit purées onto the caramel, add the mango vinegar,
then blend with a hand mixer until smooth.

Preheat oven to 430 °F (220 °C, gas mark 7-8).
Put the pineapple in a warm sauté pan and caramelize it
on high heat, turning it over several times. Transfer the
pineapple to a baking dish and make deep slits in the
flesh in several places with a sharp knife. Insert the pieces
of vanilla pod into the slits. Pour the mango juice over
the pineapple and bake for 15 minutes. Cut the
pineapple into slices and serve warm.

Maille Mango Vinegar

The beautiful yellowy-orange colour of Maille's Mango Vinegar
evokes a soft and warm world of flavours from the outset.
Its exotic flavours go naturally with fish, in a marinade or
as a dressing drizzled over leafy vegetables. Its secret is a neutral
vinegar base with generous quantities of mango purée added.
Its thick, silky texture of nectar merely intensifies the luxurious effect.
A few drops is all it takes to impart heady notes of
mango, transforming everyday meals into something
exotic, creative and uniquely flavoursome.
And for festive occasions, it adds excitement and the
unexpected to a Champagne cocktail.

Mango Vinegar is sold exclusively in Maille boutiques.

VINAIGRES DE TOILETTE
Conserves de Champignons
EAU DE COLOGNE SUPÉRIEURE
EXPOSITION UNIVERSELLE
Déposé
1855

MAISON
PAR

Popcorn in a Cone,
with Truffle Mustard

Serves 6

Preparation time: 35 minutes
Cooking time: 10 minutes

Ingredients

6 brick or filo leaves

1 egg yolk

1/3 cup (30 g) grated Parmesan

1/4 cup (60 g) cream cheese

1 tbsp (20 g) Maille Chablis
and black truffle mustard

20 g popping corn

1 tsp peanut oil

Salt and pepper

Cut each brick leaf in half. Brush one side of each leaf with egg yolk, then roll it into a cone shape with the egg yolk outside. Dip the cones in grated Parmesan. Bake in a 350 °F (180 °C, gas mark 6) for about 10 minutes, until the cones are nicely browned and crispy. Set aside.

Mix the cream cheese with the Chablis and black truffle mustard, season with a little salt and pepper. Spoon this mixture into a piping bag and refrigerate. Heat the peanut oil in a skillet, add the corn kernels and cover tightly. Cook until all the corn is popped, then take off the heat and season with salt.

Fill the brick cones with the cream cheese and mustard mixture. Arrange three popcorn kernels on top of each cone, then serve.

You can also decorate them with a slice of black truffle just before serving.

Vitello Tartuffo

Serves 6

Preparation time: 45 minutes
Cooking time: 1 hour

Ingredients

1 1/2 lb (500 g) fillet or loin of veal

1 tbsp olive oil

4 large globe artichokes

2 tbsp Maille hazelnut oil

5/8 cup (150 ml) heavy cream

3/8 cup (100 ml) grape seed oil

2 tbsp truffle juice

1/2 tsp natural truffle aroma

1 tbsp Maille balsamic vinegar
of Modena

1 tbsp Maille sherry vinegar

1 tsp Maille chablis
and black truffle mustard

1 3/4 oz (50 g) piece of Parmesan

Salt and pepper

Preheat oven to 140 °F (60 °C, gas mark 2). Season the veal with salt and pepper. Sear it in a frying pan in the hot olive oil, turning it over once, until browned. Drain the veal, wrap it in cling film and put it on a baking sheet. Bake for 1 hour. The veal should stay pink. If you use a meat thermometer, it should not get warmer than 130 °F (55 °C) at the core. Take it out of the oven and set aside at room temperature.

While the veal is baking, cook the artichokes in boiling salted water for 30 minutes. Drain, remove the leaves and choke and purée the hearts in a blender or food mill. Beat in the hazelnut oil and heavy cream. Season with salt and pepper. Spoon this purée into a piping bag fitted with a smooth, flat nozzle.

Make a vinaigrette by beating the grape seed oil with the truffle juice, the truffle aroma, the two vinegars, the mustard and salt.

Cut the cooked veal into very thin, regular-sized slices.

On the bottom of each plate, draw a strip of artichoke purée. Cover with the veal and season with truffle vinaigrette. Garnish with Parmesan slivers cut with a potato peeler.

Asparagus Cream Soup
with Truffle

Serves 6

Preparation time: 30 minutes
Cooking time: 25 minutes

Ingredients

24 white asparagus
1 black truffle (18 g)
3 cups (750 ml) crème fraîche
4 tbsp Maille white balsamic condiment
Olive oil
Salt and pepper

Using a potato peeler, peel the asparagus from top to bottom. Discard the bottom part. Trim the asparagus 3 in (8-cm) from the tip (keep the stalks). Cook them for 5 minutes in boiling salted water, then drain and throw them in iced water to interrupt cooking. Drain once more and lay them on a clean kitchen towel. Set aside 12 asparagus tips and cut the remainder into chunks on a slant.

Peel the truffle, then slice it thinly. Chop the asparagus stalks and cook them in a saucepan with the cream for 15 to 20 minutes (they should be tender when pricked with the tip of a knife). Drain and blend, adding 3 tablespoons white balsamic vinegar (keep the cream).

Divide the asparagus chunks between 6 deep soup bowls (black bowls will create a pretty colour contrast between the plates and the white asparagus cream). Season with the remaining white balsamic condiment, salt and pepper.

Pour the asparagus cream on top and garnish with the asparagus tips (after rolling them in a little olive oil).

Tip: You can also use a Summer truffle, a less tasty but cheaper species than the black *Tuber melanosporum*. In this case, just grate it over the cream before serving.

Scallops with Girolle Mushrooms
and Honey Mustard

Serves 6

Preparation time: 30 minutes
Cooking time: 10 minutes

Ingredients

6 scallops in their shells

7 oz (200 g) small, firm girolle mushrooms

6 sprigs flatleaf parsley

1 3/4 tbsp (25 g) butter

2 1/2 tbsp (45 g) Maille honey mustard

Coarse salt

Fine salt and pepper

Open the scallops and clean them, discarding the mantle and beards, but leaving the white muscle attached to the shell. Clean the girolles, trying not to wash them if possible and cutting the sandy part at the bottom of the stalk. If they are very small, leave them whole, but halve them if they are medium-sized. Wash the parsley, pat dry and chop the leaves.

Put the scallops in a large sauté pan and leave on high heat for 10 minutes. Season with salt and pepper.

Meanwhile, melt the butter in another pan. Add the girolles and sauté them, while stirring, for about 10 minutes. When they are done, stir in the honey mustard and the chopped parsley. Taste and correct seasoning.

Spread a layer of coarse salt on each serving plate and add one cooked scallop, nestling it neatly in the salt in a horizontal position. Place the girolles around the scallops and inside the shell. Serve immediately.

Cocoa Salmon,

Crunchy Salad and Celery Cream

Serves 6

Preparation time: 45 minutes
Cooking time: 20 minutes
Resting time: 45 minutes

Ingredients

21 oz (600 g) raw salmon, skinless and boneless

4 tbsp olive oil

1 lime

1 tbsp unsweetened cocoa powder

1 tbsp (30 g) Maille fig and coriander mustard

150 root celery

4 tbsp crème fraîche

1 cup (30 g) fresh New Zealand spinach (tetragon) or common spinach

1 1/4 cups (30 g) rocket

6 thin strips cut from a daikon radish, 2 1/2 x 8 in (6.5 x 20 cm)

1/2 bunch fresh coriander

1 cup (250 ml) Maille balsamic vinegar of Modena

Salt and pepper

Cut 10 1/2 oz (300 g) from the piece of salmon and cut it into three equal-sized strips. Marinate them for 30 minutes in 3 tablespoons olive oil mixed with a little salt and the grated zest and juice of the lime. Drain, reserving the marinade and coat them with cocoa powder on both sides. Put a nonstick pan on high heat and line it with parchment paper to prevent the salmon from overbrowning. Quickly sear the cocoa-coated salmon on both sides. Take it off the heat and refrigerate.

Finely dice the remaining salmon. Add the fig and coriander mustard to the reserved marinade, add the diced salmon and let sit while the other ingredients are prepared.

Finely chop the celery and put it in a saucepan. Cover with cold water, bring to a boil and cook for 15 minutes until tender. Pour off the water, add the cream, season with salt and pepper. Purée in a blender until smooth, let cool, then spoon out this purée into a piping bag fitted with a smooth, round nozzle.

Wash and drain the New Zealand spinach and rocket. Brush the radish strips with oil. Mix the salad leaves with the chopped coriander and the seasoned diced salmon. Shape this mixture into 6 small cylinders and wrap each one of them in a daikon strip. Set aside.

Pour the balsamic vinegar into a small saucepan and boil it until thick and syrupy.

Halve each cocoa-coated salmon strip. Using a brush, draw a line of reduced balsamic vinegar onto each plate. On one side of the line, lay one strip of cocoa-coated salmon, then pipe a line of celery purée and place a roll of greens and salmon tartare on the other side.

Civet of Spiny Lobster
with Dried Apricots

Serves 6

Preparation time: 30 minutes
Cooking time: 25 minutes

Ingredients

2 live spiny lobsters, 2 1/3 lb (1 kg) each

2 shallots

4 1/4 oz (120 g) dried apricots
(the sourest you can find)

3 tbsp 40 g butter

1 tbsp olive oil

1 tbsp Cognac

1/2 cup (120 ml) dry white wine

1 2/3 cups (400 ml) heavy cream

4 1/2 tbsp (80 g) Maille apricots
and curry spicies mustard

Salt and pepper

Throw the lobsters into a large pan of boiling water, boil for 1 minute, then drain and let cool. Halve the lobsters lengthwise, scoop out the roe with a spoon and set it aside in a bowl.

Peel the shallots, then slice them finely.
Finely dice the apricots.

Cut the lobsters into 2 in (5-cm) chunks.

In a cocotte, heat the butter and olive oil. Add the lobster chunks and sear on high heat. Flambé with the Cognac. When the flames have died out, remove the lobster chunks. Replace them with the sliced shallots and stir on medium heat for 2 minutes. Add the white wine, reduce on high heat until almost dry, then add the cream.

Put the lobster chunks back into the cocotte, then season with salt and pepper. Cook for another 20 minutes on low heat; the flesh should remain translucent. Drain and transfer to a warmed, deep serving dish.

Reduce the sauce until thick, then stir in the apricots and curry spicies mustard and the lobster roe. Blend. Add the diced dried apricots. Pour this sauce over the lobster and serve.

Beef Fillet
with Two Mustards

Serves 6

Preparation time: 15 minutes
Cooking time: 30 minutes

Ingredients

2 1/2 lb (1.2 kg) fingerling or new potatoes

1 straw mat for cheeses
(buy from a cheesemonger)

3 tbsp (40 g) butter

1 tbsp peanut oil

2 1/4 lb (1 kg) beef fillet (in one piece)

3 tbsp (60 g) Maille chablis mustard

3 tbsp (60 g) Maille wholegrain mustard
with chardonnay wine

Fleur de sel

Salt and pepper

Brush the potatoes under cold running water until quite clean. Throw them into a large saucepan of boiling salted water, blanch them for 2 to 3 minutes, then drain them carefully.

Preheat oven to 350 °F (180 °C, gas mark 6). Tie the straw mat at either end with string to make a sort of basket and put the potatoes in it. Season with salt and pepper and bake for 30 minutes.

While the potatoes are baking, melt the butter with the oil in a frying pan. Sear the beef fillet on all sides, then transfer it to a baking dish and bake for 15 to 20 minutes. Take the dish out of the oven, cover with aluminium foil and let rest for 10 minutes.

Brush each plate with each of the two mustards. Slice the fillet of beef and lay the slices on the mustard. Add a pinch of fleur de sel. Serve the potatoes on the side in their straw basket.

Maille Old Style Wholegrain Mustard

The name Old Style mustard refers to the original mustard
before it appeared in paste form. It is dotted with split mustard seeds,
the bark and kernel of which burst in the mouth as the mustard is eaten.
It is a very complex mustard due to a very specific blend of spices.
It is one of the special charms of this old-fashioned mustard that is
instantly recognisable. With moderate spiciness, it is tempting
to consume in generous quantities. Maille's Old Style Wholegrain
Mustard is a wonderful condiment to spice up dishes with
red meat or blended with fresh cream for white meats. It also
adds more intensity to steamed vegetables. With its abundance
of flavour and texture, many connoisseurs regard it as
a truly iconic mustard.

Saint-Marcellin Cheese
with Walnuts

Serves 6
Preparation time: 20 minutes
Cooking time: 20 minutes

Ingredients
1 cup (125 g) fresh walnut kernels
1 1/2 tbsp (30 g) Maille walnut mustard
3 thin slices of walnut bread
3 Belgian endives
4 tbsp Maille walnut oil
1 tbsp Maille balsamic vinegar glaze
3 Saint-Marcellin cheeses
Salt and pepper

Blend 3/4 cup (100 g) walnuts into a powder and mix it with the walnut mustard. Set aside. Preheat oven to 350 °F (180 °C, gas mark 6).

Cut the slices of walnut bread lengthwise, arrange them on a baking sheet covered with parchment paper and bake for 20 minutes.

While the bread is baking, trim and slice the endives. Make a vinaigrette with the walnut oil, the balsamic vinegar glaze, salt and pepper. Season the endives with this vinaigrette.

Spoon the walnut-mustard condiment into a piping bag fitted with a round, smooth nozzle.

On each plate, place a saint-marcellin cheese on its edge, propping it against a toasted slice of walnut bread. Divide the endive salad between the plates and pipe a line of walnut-mustard condiment beside the salad. Sprinkle with the remaining crushed walnuts.

Capon in a Pastry Crust,

Sautéed Fresh Mushrooms and Cèpes

Serves 6

Preparation time: 30 minutes
Cooking time: 1 1/2 hours
Resting time: 30 minutes

Ingredients

1 tbsp dried powdered cèpes
and morels

4 tbsp (80 g) Maille hazelnut and
black chenterelles mushroom
mustard

3 garlic cloves

1 chunk of dry bread

5 1/2 lb (2.5-kg) capon, ready
to cook

2 1/5 lb (1 kg) bread dough
(order from a baker)

2 tbsp pumpkin seeds

6 shallots

30 g butter

2 tbsp olive oil

7 oz (200 g) black trumpet
mushrooms

7 oz (200 g) wild meadow
mushrooms (Agaricus campestris)

7 oz (200 g) girolle mushrooms

7 oz (200 g) chanterelle
mushrooms

1 cup (100 g) hazelnuts

2 firm, fresh cèpe mushrooms

Salt and pepper

In a bowl, mix the mustard and the powdered mushrooms.
Peel one of the garlic cloves and rub the bread with it.
Carefully clean the inside cavity of the bird, rub the outside with
the mustard-mushroom condiment and season with salt and pepper.
Put the garlic-rubbed bread inside the capon.

Roll out the bread dough on your work surface. Put the capon
in the middle and wrap it in the dough, folding the edges over it.
Press to seal the dough, brushing the edges with a little water
to moisten them. Brush the surface of the dough with water and
sprinkle it with the pumpkin seeds, pressing so that they stick to it.

Preheat oven to 350 °F (180 °C, gas mark 6). Transfer the
wrapped capon to a baking sheet and bake for 1 hour, then lower
the temperature to 300 °F (150 °C, gas mark 5) and bake for
another 30 minutes.

While the capon is baking, peel the shallots and the 2 remaining
garlic cloves, then slice them finely. Clean the mushrooms, trying not
to wash them if possible and discarding the sandy base of the stalk.

Melt the butter with the oil in a sauté pan. Add the shallots and
garlic and stir for 2 minutes without colouring. Add the girolles,
chanterelles, black trumpets and meadow mushrooms. Cook, stirring
regularly, for about 15 minutes. Season with salt and pepper.
Chop the hazelnuts and add them to the mushrooms. Take off the
heat and keep warm.

When the capon is done, cut off the crust on the top, take the
bird out of the bread crust and carve it, then put the carved pieces
back into the crust.

Just before serving, thinly slice the fresh cèpes over the
sautéed mushrooms with a mandolin. Serve the capon
with the mushrooms.

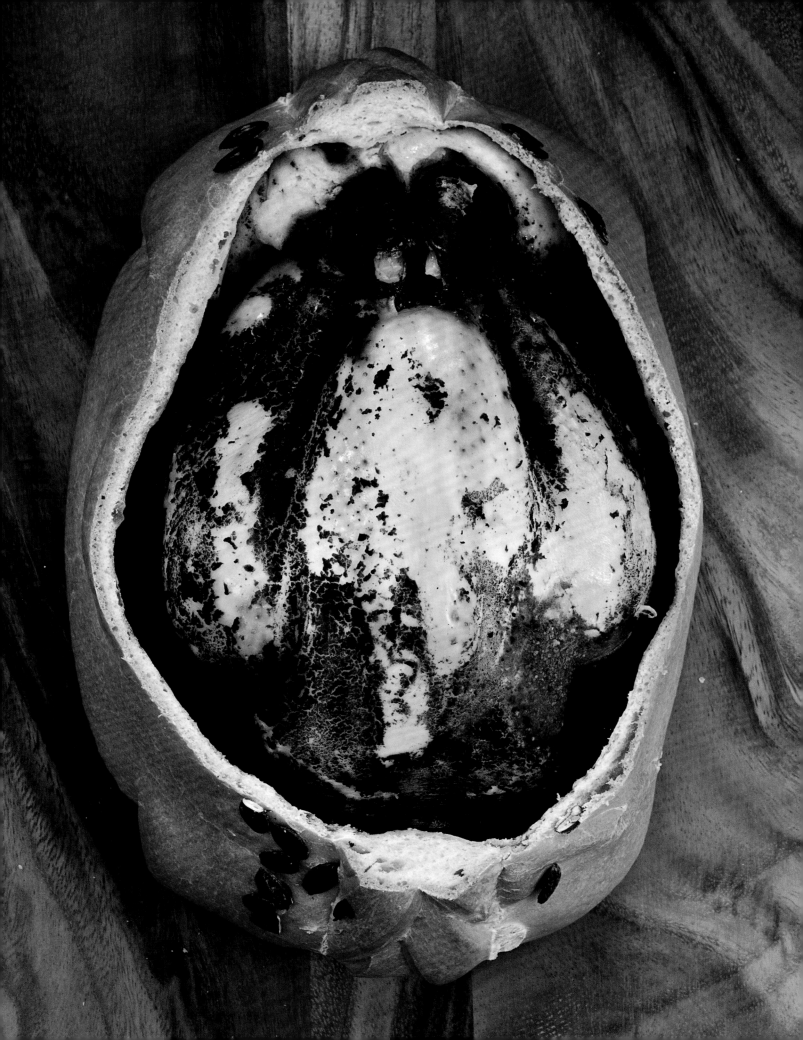

Mango Tart
with Soft Caramel

Serves 6

Preparation time: 30 minutes
Cooking time: 25 minutes

Ingredients

For the crust
2 cups (250 g) all-purpose flour
1/2 cup (60 g) icing sugar
1/8 cup (36 g) caster sugar
2 pinches powdered vanilla
1 oz (30 g) powdered hazelnuts
2 pinches baking powder
1 stick (110 g) softened butter
1 large egg (60 g)

For the garnish
1 1/4 cups (250 g) sugar
1 tbsp (15 g) heavy cream
2 1/2 leaves gelatin
5 oz (140 g) mango purée
1 stick (100 g) lightly salted butter
1 tsp lemon juice
1 tbsp Maille mango vinegar

Make the crust, mixing the flour, icing sugar, caster sugar, powdered vanilla, powdered hazelnuts and baking powder in a large bowl. Make a well in the centre and mix in the egg, then the softened butter, until you get a smooth dough. Shape it into a ball, wrap it in plastic wrap and refrigerate.

Now make the garnish. Soak the gelatin in cold water for about 20 minutes. Meanwhile, in a thick-bottomed saucepan, heat the sugar to 330 °F (165 °C) on a sugar thermometer or until you get light brown caramel. In another pan, bring the cream to a boil and take off the heat. Heat the mango purée until just warm, then whisk in the thoroughly drained gelatin. Mix half of the lightly salted butter and the lemon juice with the caramel, then add the boiled cream and the warm mango purée. Finally, add the remaining butter and cook to 217 °F (103 °C), whisking all the while until smooth. Blend in the mango vinegar using a hand blender.

Preheat oven to 350 °F (180 °C). Unwrap the dough and roll it out, then line a 10 1/2 in (26 cm) (or similar) tart tin. Cover the bottom with a disk of greaseproof paper, add dried beans or pie weights and bake for 15 minutes. Take the crust out of the oven, remove the weights and paper, then pour in the mango caramel garnish. Serve immediately.

Between Friends

Romantic Memories

Family Moments

Fine Dining

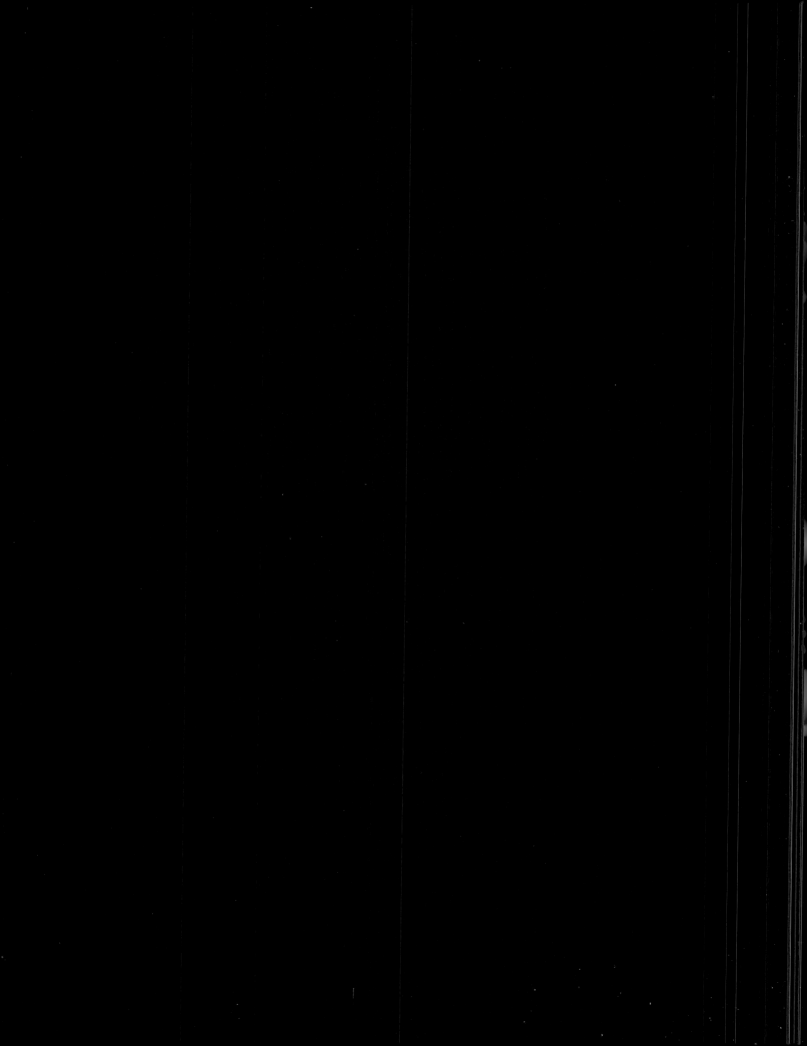

La Maison Maille sends its thanks:

*to Jean Watin-Augouard, author of the first book on Maille,
for his warm support, many recommendations, and
the historical anecdotes he shared;*

*to Potel et Chabot, and Jean-Pierre Biffi and his team,
in particular, for the culinary creativity they used with our
products and their brilliant staging during Maille events;*

*to lovers of the brand who initiated, participated in,
and gave birth to this book, whose dream has now
become reality.*

Photo Credits:

Exclusive photographic coverage by Iris Nara Miller,
with the exception of photographs courtesy of Maille House:

Pages: 8, 9, 12, 13, 16, 18, 19, 20, 21, 52, 66, 67, 68, 96, 97, 114, 115,
128, 129, 142, 143, 160, 161, 180, 181.

© Maille collection - All right reserved

Graphic design and art work:
Laurence Maillet

Original French text translated by Rob Latchford

Layout by Claire Fourmond
and edited by Primoscrib, Paris

Photo separation: APS

Distributed in 2015 by Stewart, Tabori & Chang, an imprint of ABRAMS

©2015, Published by Editions de La Martinière,
an imprint of EDLM

Library of Congress Control Number: 2014930933
ISBN: 978-1-4197-1246-3

Printed and bound in Italy
10 9 8 7 6 5 4 3 2 1

THE ART OF BOOKS SINCE 1949

115 West 18th Street
New York, NY 10011
www.abramsbooks.com